The Truth and Nothing but the Truth . . . According to Ruth

Roxanne Lord

Disclaimer: These are our recollections of events and we have tried to remain true to the stories as they were told to us.

{To Marty}

Copyright © 2020 Roxanne Lord
All rights reserved. No part of this book may be reproduced or used in any manner without the prior written permission of the copyright owner, except for the use of brief quotations in a book review.

To request permissions, contact the publisher at publishing@theavanttech.com.

Hardcover: 979-8-9869016-3-3
Ebook: 979-8-9869016-1-9

Cover art by Jett Cornelius
Photograph by Ed Lord
Book Blurb by Suzanne Sampson
Proofread by Gail Binkly

Published by Avant Tech Consulting
www.theavanttech.com

Dedication

This book is dedicated to our folks, without whom we wouldn't be here and wouldn't have these stories to tell. Our Mom did humor engagements throughout the 1980s. At the engagements she would carry 3x5 cards with notes for her stories and ask participants to pick a card, under the belief that the card picked would reveal a story that was somehow relevant for them. Thus, we had the start to this collection of stories, for which we picked cards and our brains. We have structured these vignettes in a similar manner so that they may be read randomly, with the hope that one finds their own relevancy. Stories about us were the foundation of her humor routines and we couldn't complain about it because she told us straight up, "If you can do it, I can talk about it." Though compiled and written by Roxanne, these stories represent all of our voices and memories, and they are shared with all the love and humor that defined our Mom's essential nature. The title is our Mom's, taken from her humor engagements.

The Frog Prince Lord, Mother Goose, and the Six Little Ducklings

Our Mom took a Dale Carnegie course in which they asked the attendees to list all of the things they would do differently than their parents when raising children. Our Mom turned in a blank page. When asked by the instructor why she didn't complete the assignment our Mom said, "I did. There's not a thing I'd do differently than my folks; they raised perfect children."

―――――

Our Dad was career Army. He served for twenty years, during which time all of us kids were born, and you don't feed six kids a bunch of high-cost food on an enlisted military salary. The commissary certainly helped on the cost end back in the day but when a jar of peanut butter is gone almost as fast as it's opened a big-name brand isn't on the menu, or is it? We, of course, wanted the name brand, so our Mom figured out how to get it for us; she bought one name brand container and forever after put the cheap peanut butter in it, with a little honey mixed in to bump up the flavor. Your kids crying over powdered milk? Add some vanilla to it and stick it in a "right off the farm" bottle. Your kids want the popular pancake syrup? Melt a little brown sugar into the corn syrup, put it in the popular syrup bottle. (Bonus: YOU get to eat/drink the "real" stuff to empty the containers. You wouldn't want to confuse their taste buds, after all.) Not only did we not ever catch on to the ruses, our civilian friends always wanted to eat at our house because "commissary food" was better than grocery store food.

Ya know, you just never know what is going to be someone's wake-up call. When our folks were newly married and stationed at Ft. Lewis they had a friend who'd tipple to the topple point every now and again. Concerned for his well-being and that of others, they made a deal with him that whenever he overindulged he'd find the hidden key and crash on their pull-out couch. Which he did do, and which is how he came to awaken on their couch one morning, a little bleary and a lot hung-over, and wholly dismayed to see a woman, beautiful tresses shining in the sunlight, on the couch-bed with him. What had he done? Ed and Ruth were never going to forgive him for having brought this woman (whoever she was, he certainly didn't know) into their house! Set on getting her out of there with the least amount of fuss and before our folks ever knew she was there, he reached over to awaken the lady by running his hand over her hair. That worked. She turned over and smiled at him and kissed him very sweetly. Sobered him right up, it did, as he realized, with a rather large measure of chagrin, that she was not unknown to him, she was Tammy, with whom he had spent considerable time in the past, and she wasn't going to be going anywhere as she was quite attached to our folks, seeing as how she was their German shepherd.

———

Do Moms really have eyes in the backs of their heads? Well, we can't speak for yours but the eyes in the back of our Mom's head required reading glasses on occasion, and sunglasses when it was too bright out, which is why she could be seen wearing her glasses backwards whenever she thought we needed a reminder that they were there. And yeah, they turned in our direction whenever we tried to slide out of view.

———

Our Dad had an office in downtown Tacoma where his window was at head height and ran along the sidewalk on a busy street so, anyone walking by could just look in. He kept the drapes closed to maintain privacy, which worked fine until all the drapes were sent out to be cleaned; and then it became a display window through which everyone walking past could gaze at him. He said he felt like a zoo animal, so our Mom offered to help him out with that, make it easier for him to concentrate on his work. He assumed she'd just stitch him up something really quickly that he could use for temporary blinds. It took a few passes of people pointing and laughing before he walked outside to get a sidewalk view and found that the cardboard he thought she had put in the window to discreetly block the side of his office where clients sat until she was able to make the temporary blinds was actually a sign that said, "DON'T FEED THE CPA".

When we were young kids we were not constantly supervised. We spent a lot of time on our own and were expected to exercise common sense and ingenuity, though we have to say, we didn't really expect there to be a test on how well we were doing that. We had a pick-up truck with a canopy when Suzanne and Roxanne were maybe eleven and ten, and we kids rode in the back. They came home from some trip with our Dad and were sleeping in the back, so our Dad decided to let them just sleep, come back for them later. At some point they woke up, needed the restroom, and there was no Dad in sight. The canopy had a handle on the outside, but not the inside, so they were pretty well stuck. First they tried yelling out the windows. (Doesn't matter that your Dad is very hard-of-hearing, there has to be some parental wavelength you can tap into when you're desperate to pee, right?! Maybe a neighbor?) Then they tried banging on the sides of the canopy, as if vibrations might travel better. No joy, so Suzanne finally went after the handle from the inside. She scratched her hands up good, using a lip gloss container as a hammer on the very flat lever, but got them out of there. They then went into the house, praying that no one was in the sole restroom in our eight- person household, and our Dad said, "Where in the hell have you been?!" And got their outraged, "In the truck! Where you left us! Then forgot about us!" Our Dad, "Oh." Then, "Good job getting out, Suzanne."

———

Our folks have always said that their wealth was not in their pockets, but in their children. One of the greatest gifts we ever received from them was an understanding that the ties that bind are not wrapped around particular presents, but around the rituals that create a family, or a community. Our Mom loved all of the traditions that surrounded the Christmas season that made the ordinary extraordinary, and ours started on St. Nicholas Day Eve, Dec. 5th, when we would decorate the house to the music of "Mitch Miller and the Gang", drink hot chocolate, eat cookies and then, before we headed off to bed, place our best shoes under the Christmas tree, in the hopes that St. Nick would visit us overnight. First thing on St. Nicholas Day morning, we would jump out of bed and run to the door to see if St. Nick had left a cross to indicate that he had stopped at our house. Once the cross was verified, we would go to our shoes to find them filled with the most wonderful things: fruit, nuts, books, art supplies, candy, toothbrushes, toothpaste, new socks and underwear, hairbrushes and combs. (Your own hairbrush in a house full of sisters? So great while it lasted, until someone lost or broke theirs.) You see, St. Nick brought the Christmas season, and made the mundane magical. None of us will ever eat a mandarin orange in this life without thinking of him and being reminded that joy is simple.

It must be "Pick on You Day"! Oh yeah, when we were kids and would complain to our Mom that, "So-and-so sibling is picking on me!" she'd say, "They are? Well then, it must be 'Pick on You Day'! Let's make it official and put it on the calendar." Then she would walk over to the wall calendar and write your name on the current date with a notation that it was Pick on You Day. And if you think siblings passed on that opportunity, you're an only child.

Sometimes, a kid just needs a little clarification. When our Dad retired from the Army a big party was held in our next-door neighbors' basement. At that party, our Mom made an announcement, "Master Sergeant Lord is no longer. Hereafter, Ed shall be known to one and all as Mr. Lord." On the heels of that announcement a small voice, Nannette's, asked, with much trepidation, "Does that mean we can't call him Daddy anymore?"

Our Dad, the lifelong master of sarcasm and man of few words, was a Drill Sergeant at Ft. Ord when they experienced a meningitis outbreak. (Movies have made people think of Drill Sergeants as grizzly old soldiers; however, he was twenty-six when first stationed there.) Protocol required that every other window be open in buildings when occupied, however, one of the windows which should have been open based on that metric in a building our Dad was occupying, was not. The Officer of the Day came by and ordered him to open that window. Only problem? It was a damaged window that had been salvaged by making it a fixed window, and couldn't be opened. When our Dad tried to explain that to the officer, the officer cut him off and told him he didn't want to hear any excuses, he just wanted the window open. Our Dad said, "Yes, sir!"...and put his boot through it. Glass shattered and thus the window was open, so one might have thought the Officer of the Day would be happy but no, there's just no making some people happy so, he sought disciplinary action from the Colonel against our Dad. And that's when another man of few words and an appreciation for irony pointed out, dryly, that it was a lawful order that our Dad followed. (The implication being that if he found it to be unlawful, that would put the Officer of the Day right there on the hook with our Dad.) The difference between service and servile.

———

When we were kids, a doctor told our Mom that the best way to avoid colds, flu, allergies, etc. was to keep the sinus passages moist, and told her how we should do it: when bathing, cup a handful of water and suck it up through your nose then spit it out. Our Mom called it "the hippopotamus". Sounds gross, worked fine, but is no longer advised in favor of saline solutions and neti pots or the like. As adults we were explaining the hippo to a doctor and they said, "Good God, sounds like waterboarding to me." We had to laugh and say, "Well, they were an Army doctor."

———

Blasphemy Alert
If, as an adult, Easter baskets don't tickle your fancy, then you've never received a "He is Risen" adult basket from our Mom. A clever one, our Mom, she married up exotic lingerie-shop finds with traditional Easter-basket elements in such a way that brought whole other meanings to words like, "Peep" and "bunnies" and "the toy in the egg." Yes, indeed, everything in it was bright and colorful and mostly edible---and from the local sex shop.

Our Dad enlisted in the Army when he was seventeen in order to, among other things, escape the cycle of poverty in which he was raised. Having been malnourished when he was young, he had really bad teeth, which the Army promptly removed and replaced with dentures. Now, fast-forward a couple of years to his return from Korea, during which time his driver's license had lapsed. Because he had just reenlisted, he had no current military ID, just a piece of paper that was meant to act as temporary ID until his new ID card was issued. He went into a bank to cash a bond to fund our folks 'wedding and their travel to the base he was to be stationed at. However, the teller told him that his temporary military ID was insufficient; he needed photo ID. He tried explaining his circumstances but the teller was unable to accommodate him. So our Dad, never patient with rocks and hard places (and recognizing that it was one for both of them), reached into his mouth, pulled out his top plate, slapped it on the counter, and asked if that would be sufficient as a form of ID. (Military dentures...name and ID number on them.) Cashed that bond, oh, yes she did, never mind that it wasn't strictly by the rules---and we imagine had as grand a time telling that tale as we have.

———

Until we were old enough to figure out which beverages caused the most road-trip bathroom breaks for our Dad, and thus became well-versed in the 101 reasons he'd rather have iced tea than coffee when driving, stops were rather a bone of contention between our Dad and the six female children often in a vehicle with him. He is quick to point out that he always did stop, and that is true, even if he wasn't always gracious about it. Like that one time, when we were coming home from a camping trip in our canopied pick-up and had to dig through all the gear up against the back cab just to knock on the window. Then the next thing we knew, we were bouncing around over a bad road at speeds not meant for that road and then bam, our Dad slammed on the brakes. When he let us out of the back? We were looking at the communal outhouses on the firing range at Ft. Lewis. (No toilet seats, just a long board with holes cut out at intervals.) Us, "Really, Dad?!" Our Dad, "This was the nearest restroom. Watch out for splinters."

———

Our Mom once told us that if she ever became a widow she'd act like we did as teenagers. That went over well, "You'd do that to us?!" That thankfully never came to pass but had it, we'd have had to retrieve her old mobile and put a duck with her name on it. We never had to wonder if we'd pissed off our Mom: she had a mobile with six ducks on it, our names on the ducks, and when we were on her shit list she'd cut our duck off the mobile and throw it in a drawer. You had to earn your way back onto the mobile, with a bunch of little knots on there as a not-so-subtle reminder that your duck in a drawer was just a snip away. Yes, yes, all sorts of incentive to get our ducks in a row.

―――――

Our Mom always said that her dream job would be writing dialogue for Clint Eastwood movies. Best part about it was that she wouldn't even need a team of writers, as she was sure she could manage all four words all on her own.

―――――

Take it from our Mom, people aren't necessarily uncaring or idiots, it's just not a crisis unless you realize it is. A good lesson, even if a little self-serving. Whereas our Dad's situational awareness is, as you might imagine, well developed; our Mom, not so much. She'd tell a story about how she was walking through a mall with a friend and had to step around a man who must have been really tired because he'd just lain down on the floor and gone to sleep. She didn't want to disturb him, so she made a wide path. She clued in a bit more after she heard people yelling for someone to call an ambulance. We had personal experience with it in our twenties when we went with our Mom to a restaurant for breakfast in a sketchy neighborhood. When we got back to our vehicle our Mom saw two cars facing each other, window to window for the drivers, one running and one not and she said, "Looks like they might need a jump. I'll go offer my jumper cables." Us, "Pretty sure any interference in that drug deal would not go down well, Mom." But the ultimate was when she drove our Grandma and her companion to Florida. She stopped on the road at a gas station, at night, to call our Dad. (Pay phones in those days, on the wall outside next to the door.) Our Dad asked, "Are you at a good place to stop?" Our Mom, "Yes, there are people around. In fact, a couple of young men just walked in there." They talked for a minute and then our Dad heard sirens and asked our Mom about it. Our Mom, "Oh my! There are four or five cop cars converging here." And then she started describing it all to him, "That one has a rifle." Our Dad, "That's an armed robbery going down. Get the hell out of there!!!"

———

The PIE trucks and the Culverts. On the road trip to their new home when our folks moved to Ft. Lewis the first time, our eighteen-year-old Mom saw her first PIE truck. Seeing that huge truck full of pies made her former small-bakery employee self wonder what kind of operation it would take to bake all those pies and where they all were going. And really, who's to say that the Pacific International Express truck wasn't actually full of pies? Once they were ensconced in their new home and our Mom went about familiarizing herself with the area, she started noticing cement posts all over the place with the name "Culvert" on them. Since they looked exactly like the cement posts she'd been accustomed to seeing in graveyards in Michigan (one of the services she did for family members in return for them all coming together to buy her a car when she was a teen was to take them to visit the graves of their loved ones) and she'd never seen or heard of a culvert, she thought they must be a really large family that had buried their dead all over Tacoma. She felt bad for them, that since they apparently couldn't afford plots in a graveyard they had to bury their dead wherever they could, and sad, that no one was leaving any of them flowers. And really, who's to say that culverts weren't named after a Culvert who had been buried under a cement post? Certainly not our Dad, as he was enjoying her takes on that which was new to her.

We didn't have media rooms when we were kids. We had lawn chair/sleeping bags/garage wall movies. It all started during a meningitis outbreak at Ft. Ord when our Dad was a Drill Sergeant there. Our Mom went to the library and rented a projector and movies to entertain the troops while they were quarantined. That started the tradition of her going to the library and hauling home a movie projector and movie reels on the weekends over the summers. Our Dad and the neighbor would put a big white sheet on the side of the neighbors 'garage, and the neighborhood came by for bonfire cookouts and movie nights. One summer, our Mom decided to shake things up by trying to scare all of us kids with spooky movies from when she was a kid (Bela Lagosi, Lon Chaney) but the special effects technology had moved so far that we just thought they were funny. So she gave up on that and, on a recommendation from the librarian, decided to bring home something else, meant to introduce us to a little culture. That little bit of culture gave us nightmares for months, all in about six minutes of film. Scary, creepy, bloody---horror films had nothing on it. For years our Mom told us that the director went on to become famous but since she didn't know his name, we just rolled our eyes. Well, the internet came along and we found the video, and our Mom was right: "The Big Shave", it was by Martin Scorsese.

———

When a literal-minded man runs into an even more literal-minded kid: Suzanne must have been eight years old or so and was helping our Dad get everything ready for one of the neighborhood bonfires we would have over the summers when our Dad realized he'd forgotten some things and needed to go get them. So he told her to watch the fire until he got back. And she did. She never once took her eyes off that fire. No food, no drink, hardly blinked the entire time he was gone. And when our Dad got back, she proudly told him about how diligently she had watched that fire. Our Dad, "Then how'd it go out?" Suzanne, "You told me to watch it! You didn't tell me to do anything else!"

———

We've always known that our folks valued both responsibility and independence quite highly ("Give 'em just enough rope to hang themselves up. They screw up, pull it back. They don't, keep giving them more rope.") but what we didn't know, until we were adults, was that us saying to them, as kids, "You only had me so you'd have a little slave!" and, "I can't wait to get out of this place!" wasn't having quite the impact we hoped. There's nothing like learning years later that all that drama was actually being met with claps---the ones they were giving each other on their backs since they saw such statements as proof that they were instilling in us that which they valued.

Proper usage of the word "irony"? Our favorite parental threat was always our Dad asking us, "How would you like to be walking around with a size ten and a half medium hanging out of your ass?" We just assumed it originated in the 1960s when he was a Drill Sergeant training troops. We were absolutely stunned to learn that wasn't actually true, since as a Drill Sergeant he was proscribed from threatening troops in any way, however implausibly. Which, if you think about it, makes that threat all the proof you'll ever need that being raised by a Drill Sergeant did not mean that we were treated like troops.

When Suzanne was home from college for a Christmas break she headed upstairs at our folks' place and found our Mom doing her morning work-out routine: in the raw. Suzanne, "Seriously, Mom?! Put on some clothes!" The next day she went upstairs and our Mom was doing her work-out: in socks. The day after that she went upstairs and our Mom was doing her workout: in socks and shoes. The day after that: socks, shoes, and a headband. And on and on. A private performance of the twelve days of work-out attire, right there

---

Lest we give you the mistaken impression that our Dad was the only parental badass: In the early '70s, when our Dad was deployed in Vietnam, our Mom was pulling out of a parking spot in reverse, at a stop, with a car full of kids, when a man grabbed the door handle and tried to yank it, presumably to reach in and pull her out of the car. She hit the gas, which knocked him off the car, but she couldn't reverse any further and while she was getting into gear, he jumped on the hood. She floored it, then slammed on the brakes, knocking him off the vehicle, then drove away. Once she felt safe, she pulled over to check on us and heard, "Wow, Momma! We didn't know you could drive like Daddy!"

———

One thing we can definitely say for being raised in South Tacoma is that nearly every day was an air show day! We lived under the flight path for McChord AFB when we were young, so fighter jets flying over were just a fact of our lives. Thankfully, we were post sonic-boom years, but we were not post four-across-fighter-jet scrambling years. We had to pause conversations because you couldn't hear each other. Heck, we had a huge crack in our ceiling that was obtained one day when a fighter jet was in trouble, flying so low we could see the pilot's mustache, and he had to engage the after-burners in what proved to be a successful move in saving his life, and ours. Because the jets were so loud, our Mom moved us all into the old school subterranean basement with high windows so we could get some sleep. We each had our own "stall". (As described by our Mom. We were all sleeping on old Army bunk beds, an upgrade from the Army cots we had when younger. We once had friends of the previous owners of the house, who didn't know they'd moved, come in the back door and right down to the basement. They said they knew they were in the wrong house when they saw the "Army Barracks" taking up the greater half of the basement.) The stalls were created by using cardboard wardrobes as room dividers. We also each had our own medicine cabinets. We were all perfectly happy with the arrangement as it was as close as we could get to having our own rooms. Our Mom tried to avoid the area because she knew the messiness of some of her children would drive her nuts, but she had to come down on occasion and on one of those occasions she told us, in a huff, that if we didn't get it cleaned up she'd call the Board of Health on us. And then she went shopping. While she was gone, a man came to the door and told Desiree he was from the Health Department. Being quick like she is (and desperate; she knew how many candy-wrappers were hidden under her bed), she said, "My Mom's not home and no one can come into the house when she isn't here!" and slammed the door. Then she proceeded to start issuing orders to everyone else. Oh yes, our Mom came home to the cleanest house she'd ever seen; all because in a perfect confluence of universal vibes the health inspector she was aiding in a sound study because of the jets coincidentally showed up right after she threatened to call the Health Department on us.

Deanna and her ducks: Our folks were stationed in Germany for about three years in the early '60s. Our Dad had gone ahead and our Mom and kids joined him about six months later. When our twenty-one-year-old Mom arrived in Germany she was maneuvering through the train station with tiny tots two-year-old Desiree and one-year-old Deanna, a bunch of luggage and... Deanna's ducks. (One of those deals where a bunch of wooden baby ducks were strung in a row to the mama duck and they quacked when you pulled them.) They were on a short clock to catch their train and our Mom was trying to hurry them up to find a ticket station but Deanna wasn't gonna go any faster than her ducks would quack. (Too slow they wouldn't quack, too fast they wouldn't quack.) Our Dad had told our Mom that if she ran into any problems she should go to someone with a silver---not gold---bird on their epaulettes. However, our Mom was about done with birds at that point and instead of tracking down a Colonel, she zeroed in on a cluster of young American soldiers getting ready to board a train, picked Deanna up, handed her to one of the soldiers, told him she'd be back in a minute and, before he could speak, went off to get their tickets. When our Mom got back, there stood a lone soldier holding Deanna, the rest of his unit having already boarded the train that was just moments from leaving the station. She always said she wasn't sure she'd ever seen anyone so happy to see her, and she admired the fact that even under a serious time crunch he gently handed Deanna back and didn't just toss her over. We would so love to hear the soldier's side, "That time in Germany when I was almost AWOL because some lady dropped her kid on me and there I was, standing on the platform, pulling these ducks around to keep the kid happy."

———

Our Mom never did acquire the abject respect for rank that some considered their due. When our folks were stationed in Germany they lived in an apartment complex wherein parking spaces were allotted by hierarchy. That made no sense to our Mom. She had two kids, our Dad was proscribed from carrying groceries, pushing a stroller, even holding an umbrella for her in the rain when he was in uniform (picture it. She's maneuvering all of those things while our Dad is stuck just walking along beside her), so why, she wondered, should someone else get a more accessible spot just because that someone else thought they were important? So she "borrowed" their spots when needed. And when they objected, she pointed out that she always gave them back.

———

The Berlin Wall had just gone up when our folks were stationed in Germany. Our Dad described his purpose there as cannon fodder to give the U.S. 24 hours to mobilize in case of an invasion. He would spend a lot of time in the field when they were there. Now our Mom, she spent quite a bit of time with a neighbor who was older than she, had made it through WW II. That neighbor liked to come by just to watch our Mom change the sheets and make the beds because, she claimed, she had never seen anyone do anything so slowly in her life. (Though quick-witted, our Mom was never otherwise known for her speediness.) She told our Mom, "There's nowhere to go if the invasion happens, especially at the rate you move at, so, if it ever happens, plan on popping a bottle of champagne and saying, 'Come on in, boys. Let's party!" Then after watching our Mom a little while longer she added,

"Never mind. The war would be over before you got the bottle open."

———

Having come from a family where opinions were encouraged, René struggled mightily when assigned to a particularly autocratic teacher when she was in elementary school. Ever helpful, our mom suggested the next time it was a problem that René stand, do a straight-arm salute, click her heels together, and say, "Heil Hitler." Yeah, not all the visits to the principal's office were on us.

———

Our folks met on a blind date when our Dad was on leave between being stationed in Alaska and Korea. (Well, not entirely blind, our Dad had seen a picture of our Mom. He was to attend a party with a friend, who showed him photos of his female friends, and our Dad liked the spirit he could see in our Mom's.) The friend who had invited our Dad to the party brought him by the bakery where our Mom was working so our Dad could formally ask her out. While there, the friend said something our Mom took exception to and our Mom came around the counter and kicked our Dad in the shin. Guilt by association aside, our Dad was smitten and off to the party together they went. When he went to Korea, after that short acquaintance, our Dad wrote our Mom a letter that she was not inclined to respond to. Our Grandfather told our Mom, "You owe that young man the courtesy of a response, even if it is to tell him not to write to you." And our Mom being our Mom thought, "I'll show my Dad! I'll write Ed every day." Hundreds of letters later... sixteen and eighteen years old they were at the time, the soldier and the sassy young lady.

Our folks met on our Dad's leave between what was meant to be his station in Alaska and Ft. Lewis. He assumed he'd be in the States awhile as Alaska, at the time, was considered overseas duty, and a hardship tour, and one didn't generally do one overseas tour after another, so it was with some surprise that he received orders for Korea. Anyone trying to second-guess the Army will just give themselves a headache, so he didn't think much about it until a few months later, when he was in Korea, and learned that a Warrant Officer had paid off someone in personnel to take him off the rotation and add our Dad. The issue was adjudicated and the Warrant Officer landed in the stockade. The Army, of course, considered the matter settled and didn't bring our Dad home. It wasn't an easy tour. Among other things, our Dad "rode a plane into a riverbank" and survived only because he had been bumped from his seat by someone of a higher rank. However, he might not have ever met our Mom if not for the rotation shenanigans and he definitely would not have met the KATUSA (Korean Attached to the US Army) who trained with them. Ten years later, when our Dad deployed to Vietnam the first time, he would again cross paths with that gentleman, by then a Platoon Sergeant in the elite Korean Tigers. That gentleman made it his personal mission to ensure that our Dad made it home to his family. Our deepest appreciation to him for the interest he took in our Dad and for the lesson he represented to us about fate.

Our Dad received orders to deploy as a Platoon Sergeant to Vietnam in 1967; however, he failed the physical due to hearing impairment. (What one might expect from his broad experience with ordnance: from things like being a gunner on a 57-millimeter recoilless rifle, where the rounds passed under his ear; to his years as a Drill Sergeant with no ear protection because you can't afford not to hear. It's another circumstance wherein we are grateful for what might otherwise have appeared to be misfortune as it is our understanding that the four men from his unit who alerted as Platoon Sergeants did not make it home. Instead, he and ten other men were "retread" as fuel specialists. It's work he's particularly proud of as every one of them was a combat arms specialist and they raised the level of fuel support in a combat zone to an art. And yeah, that was a rather long-winded tangent. Get over it.) That failed physical was the first time he became aware of hearing loss but that loss steadily progressed. We have a photo of our Dad from when he was in Korea that we find particularly amusing as he was the communications chief, what could be described as the ears for his unit, and the communication device he used looked like a phone. Now the phone he drags around everywhere is the ears for him. As our Mom always told us, live long enough, everything will go topsy-turvy.

Ah yes, Breatharians. If you've never heard of them, they are people who claim they live solely off the air; no liquid, no food. Our Mom, who at one time volunteered at the Psychic Energy Center in Tacoma, met a couple of Breatharians there. She told them,

"Oh yeah, I tried being a Breatharian once but I worked in a bakery and inhaling all that bread and sugar? I was putting on weight."

We had an honorary Grandma, Alice, who lived in Washington, but our other three Grandmas all lived in Michigan and we didn't know them well, so our Mom found a way to make them a regular part of our lives. At that time, Point Defiance Zoo conveniently had three bears: white, brown and black. They surely had other names but to us they were known as Grandma Aggie (the polar bear), Grandma Adelise (the brown bear), and Grandma Hazel (the black bear). We visited them regularly and heard all the family stories via the adventures of the bears. When our Mom's Ma came for a visit, we were so excited to learn that we would be going there and would get to see the grandma bears that we'd hardly made it to the bear enclosure before we started excitedly jabbering away about them. There we were, happily describing the true, but not always commendable, adventures of brown bear Adelise to---Adelise. Our folks tried some subtle gesturing to get us clued in to how what we were saying was being heard but we remained oblivious, as we had not quite yet made the connection between the person that is grandma and the bear as her stand-in. Then not-bear Adelise exclaimed,"What the hell?!" and we finally got it---since the brown bear was the only bear who cursed.

Our Mom was raised in what was a very small one-bedroom house in Detroit: she, her folks, and her brother who was near her in age. Coincidentally, it was zoned for Grosse Pointe North High School, one of the wealthiest schools in the nation. (She would say that her whole house could fit into the bedrooms of her classmates. Her Dad worked as a janitor there.) Caught between those two socio-economic worlds, our Grandma knew she couldn't protect our Mom from being the poor kid at school and the snobby kid at home but she could lessen the damage by telling our Mom, when she came home speaking the North End version of English, "Knock that shit off and talk like a normal person." As a result, our Mom wasn't known for policing our grammar. She knew language had cultural elements and her general philosophy was that any number of people could learn the rules required to edit, but having the ideas was a rarer achievement, so mostly she let errors go. But she did recognize that proper grammar has its place; like when Desiree, who didn't have a lot of experience pushing a wheelchair yet (our Mom experienced young-onset Parkinson's disease. She was fifty years old when she was diagnosed and already well progressed) was getting ready to roll her down a really steep hill in a large city with a lot of traffic and asked, "Are you in secure?" Our mom, "Darned right I'm insecure!!"

———

There was no military coverage for dental when we were kids, so our Mom had a strong interest in making us cognizant of the potential impact of various foods on our teeth. It was in serving that interest that on one Halloween our Mom took a piece of the semi-hard caramel from our treasure trove of candy and chomped into it with the intent of showing us how hard it is to separate teeth covered in caramel. And she wholly succeeded, since the caramel didn't separate from her teeth; it pulled out her filling. Point made!! She then decided to forgo demonstrating the sound a corn nut makes when you bite into one and just told us not to eat them, instead.

Before the onset of hover parenting and cell phones, parents had to be creative about how to retrieve a potentially lost kid when we were hanging out at big parks like Point Defiance. So our Mom, she put masking tape on the back of our coats with the license plate number on it. Our Dad thought that was brilliant; until he read one and realized we all had out-of-state plate numbers on our backs. (Yes, it was a joke! We did almost everything two-by-two. We can't recall a time when any of us ever got truly lost.)

In our house, if we were awakened by the sounds of our Mom's favorite musical soundtracks (Sweet Charity, Grease, The King and I) we knew there would be "chore cards" waiting for us. They were a stack of 3x5 cards with daily, weekly, or monthly chores typed on them. We had to pick as many cards as we were old for our chores (one of the many things our folks did by age) or we could get lucky and find the "free card"; the one that let you off the hook that day. Which meant, the older you were the more tasks you had to accomplish; however, also the more shots at the free card. But if it was Star Wars playing, we knew it was going to be bi-annual and semi-annual cards, full of deep-cleaning stuff we just didn't want to do. "Pick a card, any card," said Darth Vader to the little Stormtroopers.

───────

When Nannette was a tiny tot she accompanied our Mom to the doctor's office for a routine visit. While they were waiting for the Doc to come in, Nannette saw a small fly and started trying to catch it with her fingers. Our Mom sat and happily watched Nannette pursue that fly all over the room, thrilled that the fly was keeping her occupied and she wasn't having to divert her attention from all the other things in the room she might have been trying to get into. So, when the Doc came in, there was Nannette going, air-grab, air-grab, at a fly he couldn't see. He paused for a long moment and finally said to our Mom, in very grave tones, "Does she do this often?" Why, yes, and she still does; and even catches them on occasion.

───────

Though quite tidy today, Suzanne was not so much the tidy teenager. After the older sisters moved out, our family moved to a condo (with a purple door. Totally irrelevant but it's what anyone who knew us back then just said). Our folks had converted half the garage into the bedroom that Suzanne occupied. We had an inspector for something come over to our house and he was going to need to go into Suzanne's room to complete the inspection, so our Mom handed him a liability waiver she'd made to get a written release before he entered her room. He said, "I have teenagers, nothing can surprise me," and then was totally surprised when he opened her bedroom door and saw the rope tied to the inside knob. Our Mom, "For you to grab onto so you can find your way back out again." It got so bad in there that Suzanne moved her bed next to the door so that she could get to it without having to climb over a mountain of detritus. It drove our Mom nuts, so she avoided going in there. Then another sister moved out and Suzanne decided to move to a different bedroom and avoidance was no longer an option. Our Mom took a deep breath, walked into the room and realized she'd been looking at the situation all wrong the entire time and that, however unintentionally, Suzanne had saved her a nice chunk of change; no need to replace the carpet, it had never been touched. It still looked as good as the day it was laid. Having finally realigned her thinking about the upside to messiness, what was the kicker for our Mom? When Suzanne filled out her college dorm papers and requested a "neat" roommate.

———

Nature vs. nurture? Before our Mom, Desiree and Deanna joined our Dad at his station in Germany, they stayed about six months with our Mom's parents. Three adults and three small children (our uncle is six weeks younger than Desiree) in a tiny one-bedroom house. To get some space, our Grandpa liked to spend a few hours sitting outside and enjoying a beer on the weekends. On one of those respites, he set an empty beer bottle on the grass next to his chair and teething Deanna scooched herself on over there, picked it up, and started cutting her teeth on the rim. From then on, nothing but a beer bottle would do for her when she was wanting to soothe her gums. Back in the day, empty beer crates were multi-purpose and just like pretty much everyone else, our grandparents had an empty beer crate in their house. The adults were all working in the kitchen one day and trying to keep the kids out; however, Deanna kept scooching her way in there, so our Grandpa picked her up and sat her down in the empty beer crate and handed her her beer bottle. From then on, she liked nothing better than sitting in that beer crate with her empty beer bottle. Once they were in Germany, our folks took Desiree and Deanna out to eat and when the waiter asked Deanna what she'd like to drink, she said, "Bier!" Didn't get a bier that day but what is her respite beverage of choice? Uh-huh. Naturally or nurturally; she's going for beer.

———

George was a solitary bachelor who lived in the Queets and made his living maintaining the old logging roads. Our family used to go visit him for a week or so every summer. (We're pretty sure that was enough to wear him out for the rest of the year.) He would take us canoeing (and calmly pointed out, after Desiree accidentally dunked us all, the things we needed to be aware of when swimming in a river) and hiking and generally introduced us to many of the joys of simple living; to include the story about having to kill a bear on his front porch. Quite a tale for us because we knew it had to have been harrowing since George believed no life should be taken except in the absence of any alternative. None of us ever came to particularly love spiders; however, it was through George and his many webs (he never disturbed a web if he could avoid doing so, wherever it might be) that we learned all the services spiders do for people, however much we might have wished they were doing it somewhere other than where we were sleeping. (Which was all six of us in his living room, in his small two-bedroom house.) We were all very fond of that gentle soul.

The last time we saw George was in the spring on a tax-season trip our Mom took us on while our Dad was working long hours. George was elderly by then, and his eyesight was going bad. (So much so, that our mom told us not to be offended if he could not tell us apart because he could no longer see well.) While there, George decided to honor the tradition of taking us on a road tour to see a specific place on the mountain---on old logging roads---which meant narrow and cliffhanging. We were a little apprehensive because of the eyesight warning but figured, no problem, he'll ask Mom to drive. But nope, uh-uh, independent as always, George insisted on driving. It all started out well. So well, in fact, that we thought nothing of it when about three-quarters up the side of the mountain George had been whipping up, he started muttering to himself. Elderly people do that, right? Mutter to themselves? Later, we realized he was berating himself for taking a wrong turn at a fork in the road and had decided he'd just turn around right there. We certainly didn't realize it while he was muttering. Nope, we figured that one out when the backseat we were sitting on was hanging over the side of the mountain, we could feel the tires clinging to the cliff edge, and we were leaning so far forward we were practically standing up. As we're sure you can imagine, we were more than ready to scream bloody murder but we were stopped by the greatest threat known to Lord children: The Look. Yep, our Mom was giving us the look of, "If I hear one sound out of you, you will live to regret it." (Trust us...we were tempted to scream just on the hope that we

WOULD live to regret it.) As we are here, telling this tale, you can guess how it ends; with one accomplished driver whose lifetime of driving those old roads held true, and major sighs of relief when we felt nothing but solid ground beneath the tires.
We eventually left the mountain and hit the flatland. No more cliffs so nothing else scary could happen, right? Sure! Let's just keep telling ourselves that. Oh yeah, let's just kick back, look out the side windows, enjoy the scenery and appreciate the fact that on easy roads George drove like a Sunday driver. Except the scenery wasn't out the side windows, it was through the windshield, and it was a cow, standing in the middle of the road. We weren't surprised to see the cow, as George had told us he'd have to be on the lookout for them because a neighbor's fence line had fallen, so we assumed George saw the cow too, but just in case, we were getting ready to speak up and tell him about the cow when we got another one of those looks from our Mom and decided to keep quiet. All was silent in that car right up to the moment that George hit that cow. Then it was the cow talking; trumpeting her displeasure, swishing her tail, stalking off. George then turned to us and asked, "Where'd the cow come from? I never even saw her. Did you see her?" We all, of course, vigorously shook our heads no, of course we didn't see her, where on earth could she have come from? We all still laugh until we cry over that day, thinking of our Mom pointing out through her laugh tears that she'd have intervened had there been any real danger. (To us, or the cow.) Never mind that she'd left dents in the dashboard from how hard her fingers were gripping it.

———

Our Dad looks so much the same in all his adult photos that people commonly say they can't see any major changes the years have wrought. How has he accomplished this? Well, he started celebrating the anniversary of birthdays, rather than his birthday, from the twenty-second one on and apparently if you continuously celebrate the anniversary of your twenty-first birthday, you just never age. Our theory, anyway, just too bad for us that we didn't come to it before we were too old to test it out ourselves.

We rarely went out to eat when we were kids, with the notable exception of birthdays, and those odd occasions when our Mom was driving and all of a sudden the car would get a mind of its own, and no matter how hard our Mom would try to crank the wheel, the car would refuse to cooperate ("I can't make the wheel turn! The car has taken control! Where could we possibly be going?!") and rather than take us where we thought we were going, it would take us straight to a fast food joint. But really, who needs to eat out when there was such a striking array of food at home? In fact, we're pretty sure "striking" was the word our Dad's First Sergeant used to describe the bright green mashed potatoes he was treated to when our Dad brought him home for dinner on short notice. Yep, our Mom always pointed out that even though we ate our share of starches (kid fillers) that was no reason for food to be boring: if it's white, color it. Green potatoes, pink rice, blue cream sauce, purple oatmeal, a little food dye paintings on our toast. (Paint, then toast.) Though we assume our Dad's boss might have preferred a different color (green being something Army folks see more than enough of on the daily), that extensively traveled man got a real kick out of trying something he'd never had before.

———

What you didn't know about your folks CAN hurt you...with tummy-aching laughter! We were all sitting around yakking one night when our Dad made a point by saying, "Like when I tried to ride that moose when I was stationed in Alaska." To which we asked, "Wait, what???" He then told us he was crossing a bridge over a creek when he saw a moose in the middle of the creek, head down in the water. That street-smart young seventeen-year-old soldier from 8 Mile Detroit decided to hop off the bridge and onto the moose's back---where he quickly figured out he wasn't very creek-smart---one of the conclusions he reached while flying through the air on his way off of the moose's back. He said he can't lay claim to actually riding the moose, as he wasn't on there long enough, and considers himself incredibly lucky that the moose didn't see him as worth the bother to pursue after he flicked him off his back. Why did he try to ride the moose? "Because the moose was there and the bridge was close enough for me to try it. I never claimed I was brainy." In a later conversation we were clarifying and asked and then had to laugh at how it sounded, "You were an E-4 when you rode the moose in Alaska?" Our Dad, "No, Moose-riding was E-3." (Like, if you're a higher rank, you get to piggy-back on a bear or something.)
*Disclaimer: Do not try this and expect to live.

———

Grandparents! How soon they forget! Our Dad, tasked with dropping his Grandson off at school, asked him when school started. His grandson, "When the bell rings."

———

Our Mom, like everyone else's, thought it very important that we always carry a little extra hidden cash on us in case of some kind of emergency. (The ubiquitous pay phone money; though hopefully enough for a bus ticket.) And we, like everyone else's kids, often spent it on things other than emergencies. So, when she was going through a young GI's wallet she'd found to see if he had anything in there that would provide a way to contact him and she stumbled across his hidden cash, that made her so happy that when he came to get his wallet she said, "I'm glad to see that you're prepared for what may come." That young GI's face flew right past beet red and all the way to fire-engine red. It took our Mom a second and then she realized he thought she was referring to another item in his wallet, one she'd hardly taken note of: a condom. Now, it was our Mom's way to invite folks in for a cup of coffee or the like but she decided not to on that occasion, as she was doing everything she could not to appear to be laughing in his face (because she was going to be laughing her ass off, just not for the reason he might think); and to not raise any hopes that Mrs. Robinson was in the house.

———

Had you tried to tell Lord children when we were young that our folks were Santie Claus (how our Mom always pronounced it), we'd have told you it wasn't possible because we went to midnight mass every year, parents included, and Santie came while we were there. Yes, he ate the cookies, and no, he didn't drink milk. Santie drank beer. And not just any beer; he liked for you to give him a local beer. And failing to leave him a bottle opener could have such dire (imaginary) consequences that we never, ever, ever forgot. The reindeer, of course, got carrots to support superior night driving vision for the designated drivers. (Though we didn't use that term back then, we did understand the concept.) Yeah, we all still believe in Santie because how else might one describe next-door neighbors who conspired with our folks to hide our gifts at their house and then put them under our tree when we were at church?

―――――

Our Christmas tree always had a star on top; however, that was not at all a deterrent to our Mom finding a creative way to make Christmas Tree Toppers a best-selling item when she sold Christmas decorations. If you're a star person too, no problem, just put the topper on a table to add some extra Christmas spirit, or put a bunch of them out and use them to hide the Christmas "Spirits" from your teens.

―――――

Our Mom's reflections on aging, "Skinny-dipping isn't only for the young. In fact, the older you get the more you should want to skinny-dip. Why would you want to wear a bathing-suit top and pass on an opportunity for your boobs to float right back up to where they used to be?"

When very high waistlines came back in style, young people weren't the only ones wondering why. Our Mom once said to her (adult) grandson, in the way of an apology when she was late getting ready to go somewhere, "You'll never know this from firsthand experience, but when you're female and you reach a certain age, it takes a minute to get your boobs out of your belt." One of life's little realities that came home to her a number of years before that when she determined that she wanted to display her wedding dress at their twenty-fifth wedding anniversary party and went looking for a dress form. She put the word out and one of her friends called to tell her she had found one at a thrift store and our Mom okayed a sight-unseen purchase. When the dress form arrived, our Mom realized it had been made for a specific woman, of a certain age, and at that age before bras became standard. The woman the form fit was larger than our Mom and the dress wouldn't go on at all, so she dressed her in modern clothes and her boobs were stuck in the belt.

Twas the end of summer in 1970-something and our Mom was more than just a little fed up with kids. So much so that she was thrilled when she opened the yearly reminder that we needed to go in and get our booster shots. Just the thought of force-marching us through the eight miles' worth of hallways that made up Madigan Army Hospital was bringing an evil smile to her face. So she packed us all up, and gleefully anticipated the satisfaction she'd get from watching us get a jab. (She was a mother, not a saint.) Got us all into the doctor's office and the doc goes through our records and says, "Looks like only one of you here that needs a booster is Ruth Ann." Oh yeah, you know we all said, "Can we watch? Can we watch?"

———

Like many a sixteen-year-old not raised in New York City, our Mom got her driver's license as soon as she could, and then her first car. Sadly for us, it wasn't a Model T. We really wanted it to have been a Model T. We thought Model Ts were cool. We never could get why our Mom was so insistent that it WASN'T a Model T. A Plymouth it was, purchased through the pooling of extended family resources and in return for it, she spent every Sunday driving her relatives wherever they wanted to go, which was often nowhere at all, just for a ride. That Plymouth even got us a ride. Not in it, it was long gone by then. But to the library, for a book on the history of cars.

———

It's not like our Mom didn't get her own back when dealing with us as teenagers. And you can't say we didn't deserve it because really, not only did we manage to be piss-ants with our folks, we were piss-ants with each other, too. And, as can be expected, we fought most with the sister nearest in age and for Desiree, that was Deanna. So when Desiree got her learner's permit at the end of her ninth-grade year, our Mom acceded to her request to drive to school (a rare thing, as there were too many of us going too many different directions for our lone car to regularly take the place of the school bus). Desiree was at the wheel, Deanna was in the middle, and our Mom was sitting by the passenger door. As with most schools, theirs had a loading/unloading area for buses and cars. Right before Desiree entered that area our Mom bent over at the waist and put her head on her knees, making herself invisible to anyone outside the car. And in so doing, she made it clear that Desiree and Deanna truly were close and loved each other; what more proof could you possibly require than seeing them scrunched up together in the front seat with no apparent need for it?! Of course, if you'd asked our Mom she'd have gotten an innocent look on her face and said, "I know it's embarrassing to be seen with your parents at that age so I was just helping out there."

The school district asked our Mom once, and only once, what she'd do to save money in the budget. She replied, "Conduct Driver's Ed and Sex Ed in the same car."

Our Mom and Desiree took a sight-seeing road trip together when Desiree was in her early twenties. Our Mom, not wanting the obvious presence of a mother to discourage any young men who might want to wave or wink at Desiree at a stop light, decided to disguise her status by wearing a visor, sunglasses, and an allergy mask. And then she acted perplexed when less waving at Desiree and more pointing at her and laughing was going on at those lights. Now, Desiree was not altogether interested in waving at young men at stoplights anyway and was reading, instead. (Her excuse, uh story, for keeping her head down.) Our Mom, she always liked to be read aloud to, and since Desiree was reading anyway, asked her to do so. Never one to allow an opportunity to see her kids blush pass her by, when our Mom realized Desiree was reading romance novels, and trying to skip the sex scenes, she nixed that and told her she wanted word for word. And it never being enough for our Mom to just listen to a story, she commonly interjected with things like, "Ohhh, that sounds interesting!" Desiree only reads murder mysteries and true crime these days.

———

When Deanna first got her driver's license she, of course, wanted to do all the driving, but no one wanted to give up shotgun, so our Mom agreed to sit in the back seat with the little guys. She'd just had her hair done right before one of those rides and asked us to close the windows, but, no joy, everyone said it was too hot. So she took a paper bag that was on the floor, ripped out two eye-holes, and put it on her head. Us, "Mom! Aren't you embarrassed to be seen with a bag on your head?!" Our Mom, "Why should I be embarrassed? No one can see me..." Point, Mom!

———

Teenaged Suzanne once volunteered our Mom to act as a chaperone for a school field trip she was going on. Boy, was our Mom excited! A kid who actually wanted her to go on a school trip. How great was that?! And then Suzanne was so solicitous. She led our Mom onto the bus, found her a good seat, made sure she was comfortable---then exited the bus to ride on another one, thus ensuring that whatever trouble our Mom might get into, she wouldn't be there to see. And then her classmates regaled her with such fun tales of all they'd been doing on the way there, she found herself trying to find a seat on our Mom's bus on the way back but, no joy, since no one was willing to give up their seat.

Our Mom was watching a nature show with her young grandson wherein a monkey was traveling across a tree branch. This prompted her grandson to educate her on the history of evolution. Our Mom, "Well, that's half right. Those are your grandfather's ancestors. Mine were walking upright at that point."

Snow was rare in Washington when we were young, as were the homemade donuts our Dad would make on the occasional snow days. Made them in a wok, he did, the only thing ever made in our wok; which explains why too many of us were stunned and disappointed to learn, upon seeing a wok at a friend's house, that making donuts wasn't the only use for them.

We who almost weren't because of the day that almost wasn't. Our Dad was on leave before being stationed in Korea when our folks met, so they did all young men at stoplights anyway and was reading, instead. (Her excuse, uh story, for keeping her head down.) Our Mom, she always liked to be read aloud to, and since Desiree was reading anyway, asked her to do so. Never one to allow an opportunity to see her kids blush pass her by, when our Mom realized Desiree was reading romance novels, and trying to skip the sex scenes, she nixed that and told her she wanted word for word. And it never being enough for our Mom to just listen to a story, she commonly interjected with things like, "Ohhh, that sounds interesting!" Desiree only reads murder mysteries and true crime these days.

———

When Deanna first got her driver's license she, of course, wanted to do all the driving, but no one wanted to give up shotgun, so our Mom agreed to sit in the back seat with the little guys. She'd just had her hair done right before one of those rides and asked us to close the windows, but, no joy, everyone said it was too hot. So she took a paper bag that was on the floor, ripped out two eye-holes, and put it on her head. Us, "Mom! Aren't you embarrassed to be seen with a bag on your head?!" Our Mom, "Why should I be embarrassed? No one can see me..." Point, Mom!

———

Teenaged Suzanne once volunteered our Mom to act as a chaperone for a school field trip she was going on. Boy, was our Mom excited! A kid who actually wanted her to go on a school trip. How great was that?! And then Suzanne was so solicitous. She led our Mom onto the bus, found her a good seat, made sure she was comfortable---then exited the bus to ride on another one, thus ensuring that whatever trouble our Mom might get into, she wouldn't be there to see. And then her classmates regaled her with such fun tales of all they'd been doing on the way there, she found herself trying to find a seat on our Mom's bus on the way back but, no joy, since no one was willing to give up their seat.

———

Our Mom was watching a nature show with her young grandson wherein a monkey was traveling across a tree branch. This prompted her grandson to educate her on the history of evolution. Our Mom, "Well, that's half right. Those are your grandfather's ancestors. Mine were walking upright at that point."

———

Snow was rare in Washington when we were young, as were the homemade donuts our Dad would make on the occasional snow days. Made them in a wok, he did, the only thing ever made in our wok; which explains why too many of us were stunned and disappointed to learn, upon seeing a wok at a friend's house, that making donuts wasn't the only use for them.

———

We who almost weren't because of the day that almost wasn't. Our Dad was on leave before being stationed in Korea when our folks met, so they did all of their dating through letters and leaves. Our Dad promised our Mom, from Korea, that on his next leave he would take her to the apple cider mill, but when he came home, the days were passing and they hadn't gone and our Mom was certainly not going to remind him of his promise. Oh, no, promise keeping was always very important to our Mom and she had resolved that if they did not make it to the cider mill, there would be a "Dear Ed" letter in his future. (She'd just write him off, so to speak.) Our Dad, totally oblivious to what was going on in our Mom's mind, was making plans of his own (to be carried out face to face, as it were.) and would propose to our Mom at that apple cider mill. Fifty-eight years of marriage and the six of us later, we're glad it's his plan that came to fruition.

———

The stuff our Mom would stash! She once unearthed some fifty-year-old holy water from Lourdes that had traveled from France to Germany and then on every move they made in the states so that she could give some of it to the local priest. (Notice we said some, not all.) At another time, she collected sand from the Hawaiian beach that was the scene of our folks' mid-deployment rendezvous when our Dad was in Vietnam. She tried to send him some of that sand while he was still in-country but was denied by the military censors (you may not send American soil overseas) and yet she managed to get a jar of holy water all over hell and back. Huh. Guess no one wanted to mess with a Lord when carrying holy water from Lourdes which is now gracing two different houses of the Lord.

———

Who wouldn't want to live on a block where the Lord family had the Pray family on one side and the Powers on the other? Look to the end of the block and you would have found a lady named Hope. Look to the other side of the street from her and you had the McKnights, covering all of our backs. AND, once your soul was fed, you could Leggit around our block for some Franks and Stouts; possibly brewed by the Millers and consumed in Chambers. And for dessert, a mail carrier named Dilly Bar. (Yes, just like the Dairy Queen treat. We cannot recall why, except maybe because it was a sweet favorite of ours, and so was he.) Yep, our childhood neighborhood.

The Pray family were all that was gracious to a family with six rambunctious kids, not the least of which was the Thursday night beer nights Carol and Warren hosted for our very appreciative folks. (Our folks would drive us anywhere we wanted to go on Friday nights, but Thursday nights were completely off limits.) We often camped with them, and one of our favorite memories will always be seeing our Dad and Warren, two normally rather quiet and dignified men, show us just how fast they could run when the river swelled and they saw that the beer had come loose and was floating away. To give our Dad his due, there was one other time we saw him move even faster on the river; when Deanna was on a float and la-di-dahing along as if there wasn't a rocky fall coming up and failed to get out like the rest of the teens. Our Dad flew across that rough terrain and snatched her out of there like she was a whole barrel of beer about to go over.

Our Mom loved going to the movies, so when she and her grandson were out and about one day, when he was eighteen, he impulsively invited her to go to the movies with him. They went to a small theater, with only two movies available, and since they didn't know anything about either one, they randomly chose "There's Something about Mary." Yep, that kind offer would land that grandson in a theater seat next to his grandmother for a few very long hours. We're not sure we've ever seen anyone blush as hard as he did when they got home and we asked about the movie. Then our Mom, never one to let awkward dogs lie, obtained an advertising cut-out of Mary and gifted it to him as a "Movie Day with Grandma" reminder; and we all got to watch him blush like that again, and laugh. Great sense of humor notwithstanding, we're pretty sure the first app he put on his first cell phone gave a synopsis for whatever movie was currently playing at any theater in America.

———

Our Mom, when in her fifties, was awakened one night by the sound of people on their deck. She heard them because our folks slept with their slider ajar, but the open slider meant she couldn't alert our Dad (who is legally deaf) without also alerting them and since she didn't know how they'd react, thought it better to just let them leave. And they did, with all the new patio furniture. The next day she was telling their neighbor (a woman of similar age) about it and their neighbor asked why she didn't just open the blinds to scare them off. Our Mom, "Because I was stark naked." The neighbor, "Well, that most definitely would have scared them off!" We can't say we ever predicted we were going to have to talk our Mom out of doing something that might get her arrested; however, the mix of amusement and insult with which she received that statement certainly suggested she was contemplating popping up at the neighbor's window stark naked so it was a concern, right up until she said, "Meh. It would be like looking in the mirror for her."

———

As tone-deaf as we all are (and we really are), getting into any vehicle for an extended time means singing to us. (Except our Dad. He doesn't sing.) We once took a Jeep tour in the Rocky Mountains with our folks and sang our way all the way up the mountainside. The tour driver said that in his many years of doing the tours it was the most fun he'd ever had, and he was clearly sincere. It was not something he'd ever had happen before, but hoped it would happen again. We've been doctoring songs our whole lives, and he particularly liked one of those. And not that we think everything is about us or anything but hey, why not?: "The Lords go marching one by one hurrah, hurrah. The Lords go marching one by one hurrah, hurrah. The Lords go marching one by one and Roxy stops to suck her thumb and they all go marching down, to the ground, to get out of the rain boom, boom, boom. (Two by two and Suzie stops to tie her shoe; three by three and Nanny stops to climb a tree; four by four and Naynay stops to shut the door; five by five and Dee Dee stops to take a dive; six by six and Dezree stops to pick up sticks; seven by seven and Momma stops to pray to heaven; eight by eight and Daddy stops to close the gate and they all go marching…)

———

As you can likely imagine, a large family on an enlisted Army income spent our vacations camping. (People would gather to watch our Dad empty the trunk of our Dodge. There was enough stuff in there for eight people for a week. It was noteworthy.) And yes, after we finished eating our Mom's favorite version of s'mores (peel back one section of a banana. Carve out a groove in the banana flesh. Fill with marshmallows and chocolate. Replace the pulled-back piece of peel, wrap in aluminum foil, bake it in a campfire. Yum!) our tone-deaf selves spent the evenings singing around the campfire, so much joy in our off-key voices that people would come from all around the campgrounds to listen. Or, who knows, maybe it was the lyrics to the song our Mom's Ma taught her that she taught us that brought them around, "I hear you knockin' but you can't come in. I'm in my nightie and it's awful thin. I need the money but I think it's a sin. Oh well, come on in!!"

———

You might have a lot of kids if your two eldest daughters managed to harbor a runaway in their room for the better part of a week and you might not have have clued in for longer than that had they not forgotten to put away the ladder. Our folks, "We know you didn't pull it out to voluntarily do some work on the house so…"

———

Not to put too fine a point on it, but our Mom was nosy. She liked to know what was going on. However, she was totally legit about it like, no, she didn't go gossip with the neighbors or spy out our windows. She took the high road and started a neighborhood watch program, instead.

———

You can reasonably assume, besides dibs being called for that one washroom in the eight-person household miles before you got home from a road trip, that being packed into the back of the Dodge like sardines was just a natural function of family size. (We were so tightly packed that we'd fall asleep with our heads on each other's shoulders and when someone would get a crick they'd say, "switch" so we'd all switch to the other shoulder. With Deanna definitely by the window so she wouldn't puke on the rest of us.) However, time might make you reevaluate that. When Desiree and Deanna were near to moving-out age our folks bought a Pinto, so the experience was the same, even when we were down to four at home. Then a small pick-up when René and Nannette were near to moving-out age and same again, even though we were down to two at home. And that's when Suzanne and Roxanne started catching onto a theme, and figured when the motorcycles made an appearance, their days at home were numbered.

———

Our Dad has never been issued a speeding ticket though he did come close once, when all of us were very young. The police officer pulled him over, looked in the car, did a double-take, and then started counting children. He said, "Buddy, you have enough problems already. Just slow it down." It's truly been both our pleasure and our privilege to be his problems.

———

Our Dad was known as a good driver. In fact, he had to go to traffic court in mid-life from an accident where someone had hit him and the judge saw his spotless driving record and asked, "Are you a Communist or something?" Well, he didn't necessarily come by that trait naturally. When our folks were newly married they were driving through an incredibly bad storm, the visibility went down to zero, and our Dad ran into a wayward pole that was in the middle of the road. Our Mom? She was glad no one was harmed and felt bad about the condition of the car but that didn't mean she was going to run the risk of anyone thinking she had crunched the front end so at the first opportunity she took a can of spray paint and wrote, in big block letters, "HIS" over the damaged portion. He never hit a thing after that.

———

Our folks were always down for a road trip. Our Mom loved them so much that she'd let us pick the music, even when she was driving. (Proof, beyond a reasonable doubt.) She would say that she was like a dog, open the door and she'd climb in. In their retirement years she liked to map the trips to make sure we'd go by her favorite spots, all coincidentally ones with legal gambling. (Bonus if they also had shows, which she really enjoyed.) If we were within three hours of Las Vegas, we were going through Las Vegas. If we'd remark on it she'd say, "What? Are you in a rush?" It was so predictable that we thought they should change their slogan to "Wherever you are, you're close to Vegas." But not all their road trips were for pleasure. Throughout our lives, we made many the detour to see someone safely on their way. At Ft. Lewis, our folks drove a lost sailor who'd found a military base, though not his military base, back to Bremerton so he wouldn't be AWOL. In Germany, our Dad was on courtesy patrol and rather than turn a drunken soldier who'd just received bad news in to the military police, he and our Mom pulled Desiree and Deanna out of their beds, wrapped them up, and put them in the car with them to drive the man to his home in another town. Those are just two of the many such journeys that occurred across the span of many years. And yes, we did deliberately omit the Las Vegas one since, at least for now, it's still "What happens in Vegas, stays in Vegas."

———

For Roxanne's graduation from The Evergreen State College (also our Mom's alma mater) our folks took her on a trip to Kauai and René decided to join them. Renés not much of one for just kicking back and doing nothin' so while there, she decided to take surfing lessons. She thought she'd be a little nervous about trying it out in front of so many people (the beach was pretty full that day) but really, no one but family was taking much notice of her. Which was good, since only our Mom realized that on her last run she not only steadily gained the board, she was looking to come all the way in; minus her bikini top. Our Mom, ever helpful about heading off a potentially embarrassing situation, yelled out to René that she had lost her top. But, René was too far out and didn't hear our Mom, so our Mom yelled a second time; and thus assured everyone on the beach that they had heard her correctly the first time and that there actually was something to be seen, other than the horizon, if they looked out toward sea. René, a little disappointingly to her, wiped out before she made it all the way in; then wasn't nearly as disappointed when she saw her bikini top floating on the wave in front of her. (Duck and cover becoming, right then, one of the more useful things she ever learned in school.) Indomitable, René said, "Well, I got the hang-loose part down." And really, you couldn't claim she wasn't getting into the spirit of Roxanne's graduation since Evergreen's motto is, after all, Omnia Extares----Let it all hang out.

―――――

What do you do when you no longer have a bunch of kids to play musical dining-room chairs with every night? Well, if you're our folks, you start playing musical dining-room table and chair sets. It all started with a dining-room set our Mom was looking to purchase, but the sales people would not give her the "everything included" display vase and flowers, and they were rude about it, so she walked away, decided it wasn't the set for her. After that time they bought, we think, six different sets. We swear, it was like they never saw a set they didn't buy. Roxanne and her husband Marty were driving home one night and Marty looked at a neighbor's house and said, "Didn't he have a dining-room table in the yard for sale this morning?" Roxanne: "Yes, he did. My folks probably bought it. Haha, just kidding." They got home, and the table was on the back deck, waiting to replace the one in the dining room. Yep, they even caught our folks sneaking out to "look at" dining-room table sets. They had to ask, "Do we need to start looking for a dining-room set interventionist?!" Our folks did finally find one they liked---and moved on to place mats.

When your kids are grown and you're ready for new challenges, but not new headaches. We can all unreservedly attest to our Mom's exceptional skills in all areas listed, particularly as a companion.

Surrogate Leisure Time, Inc.
Ruth Lord
Professional Surrogate (Stand in for)
The psychology behind my surrogate occupation is that you feel terrific about giving someone else (me in particular) an opportunity you can't take time to enjoy yourself. Your wise decision to hire me, a surrogate, eases your guilt feelings and reduces your stress. You are, after all, providing an opportunity for your fellow human being (me in particular).
I take vacations for you when you don't have time to go for yourself. I am a companion for you when you don't want to travel alone. If you have a fear of flying, I'll fly for you; if you get seasick, I'll take a cruise for you.
I also attend breakfasts, lunches, and dinners that you really want to attend but can't fit into your busy schedule. I attend classes, meetings, seminars, conventions, and conferences for you when you have a conflict in engagements.
I do volunteer work in your name. I attend your church

services. I visit your friends and relatives. I exercise for your health (my choice of exercise).

I do select research projects, take pictures and write letters. I read books for you that you just can't get to; I just lie on the beach for you.

Plus I attend concerts, plays, ballet, and even movies for you. You only have to ask, and I critique videos for you.

I will not do anything that conflicts with my personal code of ethics and/or morals. I reserve the right to refuse service to anyone without explanation.

Motto: "Life is too short to take it seriously; so if it's not fun I'm not doing it for you."

All expenses are incurred by the client.

Fees are negotiable.

Reservations are recommended due to the popularity of the surrogate.

Franchises are available.

Copyright 1992 Ruth Lord

———

We could be little pukes when we were young. We sassed, we sulked, and we could be pains in the ass and make a big production out of being told what to do but what we didn't do is we never, ever, questioned our Mom's instincts. You're all standing on the lower deck of a ferry to get some air and Mom tells you to stay behind the glass? Even though the point of being out there was to get some air? You stayed behind the glass, and thus missed being hit with the spray when someone on an upper deck hurled over the side of the ship. Vomit hitting the window instead of your face as it did other people's? Guaranteed future compliance.

———

Back before the exhortation was common, our Mom used to tell us to to think of five things before we went to sleep for which we were grateful that day. Our version of nightly prayers. We've never seen much reason to quibble over the description when it comes to good fortune: God, Gods, Divine Providence, the Universe, sensitivity, instinct, coincidence, luck. As far as we're concerned, call it what you will, we're just happy for good endings. And many of those good endings were attributable to our Mom always trusting her gut. For instance, our folks moved into an RV for a few years and our Mom drove from Washington to Colorado in their car with a U-Haul trailer and our Dad drove the RV. They were crossing a pass late one night and our Mom, with no logical reason for it, decided to move into the left lane. She said, "I don't know why, I just did." Our Dad, having trusted our Mom's instincts for many years, crossed into the left lane after she did. At the next bend in the road, there was a giant dead elk in the middle of the right lane. There was no real reaction time once they'd seen it. Had they been in the right lane, and been lucky, it would have totaled at least one vehicle. If they were unlucky, it would have sent them off the side of the mountain. Pretty sure our gratitude was clear, whatever the source of the good fortune.

Our Mom disliked the heavy bass of hard rock music, particularly when it was shaking the floors she was standing on from below. She got tired of running down the stairs to get a volume drop so one trip over her limit, she tossed all of Suzanne's records. Then she felt guilty for not finding a different solution and sought to make amends by offering to replace them. Suzanne, recognizing that she bore some of the blame, thought it would be nice to offer a compromise and asked for Kenny Rogers albums. They were something she thought they could enjoy together. And in a heroic act of good faith, she really really tried to enjoy the Conway Twitty our Mom mistakenly purchased in their stead, but it just wasn't the same.

―――――

We had a mentally ill neighbor for a time. If you didn't lock your doors, he'd just come in your house, make himself at home. He always claimed that he worked for the whole alphabet soup of federal agencies: NSA, CIA, FBI, DEA, etc. It all sounded a bit unlikely to us but then one day our Mom showed us a newspaper article about a "spy summit meeting" where all the attendees were pictured and named in a pyramid of rank. The only photo missing was the top dog but his not-uncommon name was listed and, it was the neighbor's name. Huh.

―――――

Our Mom instituted weekly family conferences when our Dad was deployed in Vietnam because she was tired of always being the bad guy and wanted us to see, and participate in, the practical functions of family: tasks that needed to be completed, budgets, discipline, etc. Those family conferences would continue throughout the time we lived at home. How does a family conference work when you have a House of Lords? And a really unbalanced majority? Well, our Dad (otherwise known as the Democracy of

One) served as family conference President for unlimited terms. A well-liked President, but often called upon to make unpopular decisions. Our Mom, the Supreme Court of the family conference. She could see your point of view and still squash you like a bug when you tried to make unfamilystutional moves. The rest of us? Congress, our state of mind determining how we were going to represent the body politic in the House. Those are the facts; citizen (not subject) to some interpretation.

———

Our Mom liked to audio-tape things (our weekly family conferences, her humor engagements, letters to our Dad when he was deployed, etc.) so we have a few tapes of how family conferences went. When Desiree turned eighteen, our folks were laying out, at a family conference, her new rights and responsibilities and teaching her about credit and all that. (Desiree, "Do I actually have to spend money on the credit card to build credit?" Wait, what?! Desiree not wanting to spend money? Or was it Desiree seeing a great excuse to do so?) Pretty dry stuff that was apparently being heard as, "Blah, blah, blah" by a younger sibling (we don't know who since the tapes are just audio) because in the middle of one of our Dad's sentences you all of a sudden hear our Mom say, "SIT DOWN!" Trying to creep away from the table because you're bored? Not happenin'.

———

We all had a say on the disciplinary front at our family conferences when someone was being called out for misbehavior. Our folks would go around the table and ask us what we thought would be the appropriate response. Suzanne and Roxanne always said, "Spank 'em!" for the other sisters (a bit gleefully, a bit meanly; drunk on their own power) till...oops...they met the bitch that is payback and it was their turn for folks to offer up disciplinary actions for their behavior. Our Mom commonly left the table during those discussions and went to the bathroom. We thought she just had a weak bladder but learned later that no, not a bladder issue; she had to leave because she'd get the giggles about what was going on (like the stunned and outraged expressions Suzanne and Roxanne would get when someone would dare propose they get spanked. Us? Angelic little us?!) and would have to leave to recompose herself.

―――――

Spanking was a disciplinary measure commonly used in our day. (We would be swatted as many times as we were old. As with other stories found herein, yet another of our folks 'age determined numbers.) Now René, she never cried when she was spanked. Not ever. Suzanne was so in awe of her fortitude, she asked René about it. René told her that she would put on a second pair of underwear before a spanking, add a little extra padding. (Our swats didn't come out of nowhere, we had notice.) Suzanne thought that a great idea but decided to do her one better the next time she crossed the spanking line and shoved all of the contents of her underwear drawer into her pants. Our Mom saw her lopsided butt and asked about it. Suzanne explained to her that she didn't want to cry and René told her this is how you do it. Our Mom laughed so hard that Suzanne got a free pass on that one.

Among other things, we used family conference time to get our schedules in order for the week. Our folks encouraged us to give them options since there was always so much going on that we sometimes needed creative approaches. And a very young Nannette definitely took that request seriously and went out of her way to give them options, as demonstrated in a note she once wrote to our Mom:
"Dear Mom,
Please pick me up at twenty to four or 3:40.
Nan"

Among the many personal things our Mom audio-taped, we found a taped Wayne Newton concert. We said to our Dad, "Dang! Mom illegally taped Wayne Newton?!" Our Dad, "It was prohibited to tape at the Wayne Newton concert she attended, however, she made security aware that she wanted to tape the show to send to me in Vietnam and they sent word up the line and Wayne Newton approved it." For those who've ever wondered about Wayne Newton's enduring popularity...there ya go, one more reason.

Whenever one of us talks about our Mom audio-taping letters to our Dad when he was deployed, someone invariably says what a great idea that is and it's too bad they can't think of anything to tape. Well, our Mom also read books on tape to her grandkids.

We're strewn all over the country so it was a way for her to read them a bedtime story. Yes, you can buy/download audio books for kids these days but it's not the voice of a loved one reading it.

———

You were definitely a military brat if: your superhero jammies were your Dad's old Army green t-shirts.

———

In our experience, people tend to have a lot of misconceptions both about what it's like to live in a household with all-female children and what it's like to be a Drill Sergeant's kid (Our Dad trained troops at Fort Ord, California, from early 1964 to late 1967), and strangely, those misconceptions tend to run down similar paths: we were well-behaved, always had a tidy house, lived by rigid routines, got yelled at a lot. But, not so much. We were pretty much just like everyone else, with the primary exception being that we didn't know anyone else who was raised by a Drill Sergeant so we found ourselves explaining things like, no, our Dad didn't bounce quarters on beds and he wasn't given to raising his voice. He didn't do it when training troops, didn't do it with us. He was all about withering us with a look. So much so that we'd tell people, when they asked why none of us ever joined the military, that we didn't think we'd be able to make it through basic training without asking a Drill Sergeant who tried to give us a look, "Seriously? Is that the best you got?" Which is not to say that none ever considered it. We admired our Dad, so much so that Desiree looked into ROTC when she went to college. However, there was a bit of a misunderstanding when she was told she needed to speak to someone with authority to deal with her questions and, being an enlisted Army brat as she was ("Don't call me sir, I work for a living"), she made an appointment with the Master Sergeant (a non-commissioned officer) rather than a commissioned officer and when asked why by an officer, she said, "Because I wanted something to get done." And with that statement she did get something done, she convinced the hierarchy that she wasn't likely to be a well-behaved, tidy, rigid cadet and that maybe she'd prefer to choose other avenues in her future career.

We had a good-sized yard when we lived in South Tacoma. The front yard had a pond, the back yard had a large field of grass. Our Mom managed to eradicate any grass from the front by turning it into a park-style rock garden. (We kids moved an hour of rocks every day we got home from school until it was done. And boy, did we ever complain!! We likened it to hard labor for crimes of which we hadn't been convicted; but surely did.) And not one to forget our furry friends, our Mom even turned the area between the sidewalk and the street into a pet "Rest Stop", with some hope that other people's pets wouldn't be dumping any new "rocks" in our garden. It was the back yard that remained a bone of contention. The camp fire pit we had was great but the rest kept going to pot because no one in our family liked to mow and our Mom just could not keep enough rabbits and guinea pigs around to chew the grass down. Our Dad complained about it before he was set to leave for a trip. He told our Mom they needed to do something about it. So, she did. While he was gone, she went and bought a pool and had it installed. (Thank you, Mom!) He came home to problem solved! It was great. An above-ground pool with four feet going below so we had eight-foot depth on one end, and a dome over the top. Our Mom worked some serious magic to make it happen. Our next-door neighbor worked for Coke and he made a deal with the older sisters to babysit his kids and in exchange he'd let us use a pop machine. We had such a great time with that pool until it popped and the soda-pop pool dried up that it will forever define our general ideal of yard work; swimming with a drink in hand.

———

Our folks often talked about what very good years they enjoyed at Fort Ord, where our Dad was a Drill Sergeant in the mid to late '60s. It was a strong community, and our Dad had not yet deployed on his first tour in Vietnam. They made life-long friends at Fort Ord: the Freedle family. Ann is a smart, energetic lady who understands how to motivate people to reach deeply into their pockets for a good cause. With that goal in mind she organized a fundraiser, through the NCO Wives 'Club, that caused our Dad to be a rather attractive bridesmaid (though sadly, never a bride) at an all-male wedding. The wedding party was wholly peopled by a bunch of gritty soldiers, our Dad in a lovely red frock. Even though they all knew it was a marriage of convenience, there was not a dry eye in the house at this wedding; seeing as how everyone laughed so hard they cried. Hankies galore when the ceremony concluded and the bride (Special Forces) carried the groom off into the sunset.

———

It was just Suzanne's bad luck that our Mom was a strong believer in answering any and all questions until no questions remained and, that she was just coming out of the shower when Suzanne decided to ask her about the hemorrhoid cream commercial she'd seen. Since our Mom's verbal description of hemorrhoids failed to get the concept across, our Mom bent over and showed her. And just like the that, our Reader's Digest Great Encyclopedic Dictionary became a good investment that was guaranteed some future use.

———

Even with all the movement of people to and from military bases, it does end up being like one big neighborhood family, whichever base you are on. And we're not just saying that, we can prove it. For instance, when we lived on Ft. Lewis the last time, older neighborhood kids came by and asked our Mom if they could take Nannette and Suzanne to the park; give her a little break from kids. They got up on the teeter-totter, Suzanne on one side with one of the older kids, Nannette on the other with the other. When the kid on Nannette's side was done teetering, he and Nannette tottered off the teeter-totter--- when they were on the ground side tilt. And, the teeter-totter did what teeter-totters do: slammed down. In this case, right onto Suzanne's foot, and broke it. (Ouch!) After a few days of Suzanne hobbling around in her cast the older siblings felt sorry for both our Mom and

Suzanne, her being stuck in the house and driving our Mom to distraction, so they decided to offer Suzanne a distraction and take her out and pull her around in the wagon. A little while after they left our Mom looked outside and saw that the elders were pulling Suzanne in that wagon all right---tied to the back of their bicycles. She had just made it to the door and was getting ready to yell when that there wagon went flipping over and gave Suzanne a concussion. (No, we're not laughing. Really!) See, family! Decide to help Mom out, mayhem ensues.

―――――

In our family, one of the responsibilities that went with the privilege of gaining our military ID cards at the age of ten was commissary shopping with our Mom. A real job, that shopping was: groceries for eight collected on one day of the month. (And then we pigged out on all the fresh stuff. Even now when we overeat we can be heard to say, "Man! I ate like it was commissary day, today!") The accompanying kid's responsibility was pulling the coupons out of the red coupon wallet as they walked through the aisles, matching the coupons to the items. It was a rite of passage for us, cloaked in mystery until you gained the age to go yourself. Our reward? A chocolate soda, picked up last, and a treat that was solely reserved for having gone shopping with Mom. And, going shopping gave you a pass on putting away groceries and making what felt like a gazillion hamburger patties to set them up for freezing. Our Mom was no dummy, she knew exactly how to make us yearn for the day we could walk the aisles and fill up the four huge shopping carts with her.

―――――

Our Mom liked to say that Roxanne's early admission to college was actually a reprieve she got from kids for good behavior. But the truth of the matter was, it was more like work release and a halfway house. Roxanne wanted to be "independent" and earn her own spending money so she kept her weekend job in our home town and our folks did the 45-minute drive down to her college town to pick her up on Fridays and drove her back on Mondays. (Our Mom got a real kick out of the program course Roxanne was taking. At the end of her humor routine our Mom would often say, "Do you have any questions? I can answer questions." (Usually met with silence.) "Do you have any answers?" (Met with laughter.) Then, "The daughter at Evergreen took a course called, 'Great Questions and Great Books' and I said that's a perfect course for her because she's had all the answers for years.") So, time behind the wheel=x dollars. Gas=y dollars. Wear and tear on the car=z dollars. Roxanne's income=negative xyz. Bringing your sixteen-year-old kid home every weekend their first year to make the transition easier? Priceless.

Really, don't ask if you don't want to know. One of our folks 'granddaughters (twenty-four years old at the time) drove our folks home from a trip they took and was helping our Mom put her stuff away and found a quarter lodged in the bed. Granddaughter, "How'd that get there?" Our Mom (casually, but surely with a devilish gleam in her eyes), "Oh, your Grandfather throws them at me when he wants me to dance." Granddaughter, in a shocked voice, "Grandma!!!!" And thus a new generation learned that what you don't know can't embarrass you.

―――

Like parents do, ours were happy to lend a hand whenever they could. Roxanne owned a small paperback bookstore for a number of years and our retired Dad would sit in for her whenever she couldn't be there. In recognition of his contributions, she gave him a 100 percent raise every year. Picky CPA that he had been, he was quick to point out that 100 percent of nothing is still nothing, but truly, what amount of money could cover just how priceless it is to have someone in the bookstore who answers the question, "Is this a good book?" by saying, "How should I know? I don't read that trash."

―――

Unlike our Mom, who always liked comfortable clutter, Roxanne is a minimalist by nature. When we were kids, we'd do a week long Goodwill sort once a year and our Mom would always have to go into Roxanne's bag and take things back out and tell her she needed to keep them. It always amused our Mom that when she bought a twelve-year-old Roxanne a puzzle book to take with her on a trip, Roxanne tore out the pages that interested her and gave the book back so that it wouldn't take up space in her bag and someone else could get some use out of it. Not at all the way our "just in case" Mom would have approached it, and the reason our Mom prevailed upon Roxanne to help her sort many times over the years. At one point, Roxanne converted the small bookstore she owned into a tourist shop and whereas it's a good thing for a bookstore to be highly organized, it's not nearly as desirable for a tourist shop, so it was with some satisfaction that our Mom agreed to her request to turn the table and help her set up the shop. However, she was cognizant of Roxanne's preference that everything in the shop have a useful purpose and that if she didn't see a useful purpose for something she'd likely take it out of the shop, so our Mom suggested alternate ways to use various items. For instance, Roxanne's husband, Marty, built a tower out of the bookstore wood for the stickers Roxanne would be selling but they were a little concerned it wouldn't work out so our Mom pointed out how well it would also work as a dancing pole. The wood would still have a purpose, and tourists would really get to see a sight. And then she did a nice little dance around the shop pole to prove it.

When there's one blonde amidst the sea of brunettes: Some years ago, when we were all teenagers and up, our folks started going out on their date nights to a really nice restaurant; a place they enjoyed for good service and unobtrusive staff. Our folks enjoyed themselves there so much, and the staff enjoyed them so much, that it was decided that our Dad would take each of us daughters, independently, on a "get dressed-up father/daughter dinner night" at that restaurant. We went chronologically so Desiree was the first to join him. Some eyebrows raised when he entered the restaurant with her, but he really didn't think anything about it. A little later it was Deanna's turn; eyebrows went up, and service at their table became a bit abrupt. Then a lone dinner with our Mom that brought a bit of a cold breeze his way and our Mom the best service she'd ever had. A little after that it was René, and service that bordered on outright rude. That's the dinner when our Dad clued in on the problem as the hostess asked, "Oh, these are your daughters, aren't they?" Never in a million years, without that question, would it have occurred to our Dad that anyone would assume those dinners were anything other than what they were. And our Dad, being our Dad, would have felt no compulsion to set anybody straight once he did learn they were drawing conclusions that had nothing to do with reality but fairly assumed that the hostess would settle the matter and the service would be fine again. Which she did do, but only after our Dad showed up with THE BLONDE. That was apparently more than the wait staff could stand as service that had bordered on outright rude became downright hostile. To avoid someone dumping food down the "Homewrecker's" dress the hostess had to go into the kitchen to make a general announcement. (And how they knew Homewrecker was Nannette's family nickname, from when she was small and into everything? We'll never know.) Suzanne and Roxanne? Proved the theory that younger children are always spoiled and had perfectly wonderful dinners.

———

Never let it be said that our mom was anything other than an indulgent parent .There're so many things she would have done with us that no adult in their right mind wanted to do; if not for that bone in her leg. Yep, when we were really small and asked her to do something she didn't want to do she'd say, "I'm sorry, I can't do that. I have a bone in my leg." We'd go whisper (like saying it at a regular volume would somehow make it worse) "Ooohhh, Momma can't do that, she has a bone in her leg."

———

Nope, not a one of us has ever felt any need to go on one of those TV shows where you prove you're a glutton for punishment. We've already proven our fortitude by conquering the challenge of eight people and one bathroom: creative shower peeing as a solution to pressing problems; the list on the bathroom door René made up allotting everyone (folks included) a use-it-or-lose-it shower time; our Dad grabbing a newspaper and thus causing a run on the bathroom before he could get in there; the eight people in line after a long road trip. We're getting all leg-crossing sentimental just thinking about it.

———

Ah, Cookies for Nookie:
Our folks were stationed in Germany when the Berlin Wall went up, so our Dad spent a lot of time in the field. There was a curfew in Germany at the time so it was an infraction to be on the roads after dark. (At least for American military and dependents, we don't know about anyone else.) But love will find a way so our Mom used to drive out and meet our Dad, in the woods, after curfew, when he was away from home for long stretches. And never, not once, paid a penalty for it. Not because our Mom was never stopped; she was. And not because she's not the one who'd have actually paid the penalty, since military culture at the

time made service members wholly accountable for anything their dependents did, as no charges were ever levied. (If our Mom had ever received a traffic ticket, our Dad would have been required to go to driving school, and she would not have. If a check was bounced, it could have cost him a grade.) Nope, it was because she set out for those rendezvous with freshly baked cookies---lots and lots of cookies. Turned out to be her absolute get-out-of-trouble-free card. "I'm so sorry. I know I'm not supposed to be out after dark. Would you like a cookie?" And we have René as the result. So, take it from someone who's lived a little: never underestimate the value of good cookies.

———

Our Mom took a body-language reading course once and then a friend asked her to read her body language. Our Mom studied her for a minute: a tall lady, too tall for the chair she was sitting in, so she was all twisted around. Our Mom, "I'm sorry to have to tell you this but you are suffering from an ancient disease: Lack-a-nookie." The woman, recently divorced, figured that was an illness she'd not be able to address anytime soon so our Mom advised her to hit the kitchen before either of them started suffering that other ancient disease: Lack-a-cookie.

———

It's an undeniable fact that Lord children are door slammers. You never have to wonder when we left or when we've arrived, a resounding echo will tell that tale. What else might you expect from a bunch of kids who thought we'd sneak out and play one night when we were supposed to be quietly entertaining ourselves in the living room while our Mom was helping the neighbor with something and we got totally busted because in our quest to be quiet we didn't quite get the door shut all the way and a skunk came by to sample the popcorn we'd left in a bowl on the floor? Being stuck outside and waiting for your Mom to get back and turn your ass into grass (because we were actually smart enough to recognize that the only thing worse than the restriction we were going to get was trying and failing to do it ourselves, which would get us stuck grounded in the house with pee-yew!!) is a pretty guaranteed way to train you into ensuring any door is fully closed.

―――――

It's interesting to us how often people have thought there was some kind of incongruity to our Mom's involvement in promoting the Equal Rights Amendment in the early '70s because our Dad was career military. To us, there is no disconnect between the two. Yes, it's true that while our Mom was busy at the offices the in-house baby-sitters for us kids were self-described militant lesbians. So what? They took great care of us. And our Dad has always been of the philosophy that defense of our ideology is the duty and privilege of all of us. He would say, "In my life I have had to rely on people of every race, religion, sexual orientation, what have you, to pick up a weapon and guard my back, to bind the wounds of the injured. I, and many others, are here today because they did. End of story." All he cared about was honorable service. And as far as our Dad knows, his unit was the first to take female soldiers into the field at Ft. Lewis. That made him the first sergeant to do so, and to see them surpass all expectations. He was always of the belief, "Prove that they can't. If you can't, they can." Concerned about women on the front lines and menstrual cycles? Our Dad, "What, are there bears on the other side?" So, no, no conflict. Though maybe a raised eyebrow on occasion for some of the militant things his kids came home saying after a day at the ERA offices with Mom.

In the early '70s, our Mom actively worked on the Equal Rights Amendment. At that time, she got a burr in her bonnet (yep, just mixed idioms...sue us) about how the only directions girls were being taught to follow were cooking recipes and sewing patterns. So she went on a model kick, and bought each of us kits. We thought they were great, right up until she wanted us to gift models to our girlfriends on their birthdays. We balked at that. In what world was a model kit going to go over well at a birthday party for some of the girls we knew? But it wasn't up for debate, and even trying to "forget" the gift at home so we could give it later, not in front of anybody, was a lost cause since our Mom always asked if we remembered a gift. And those model kits ended up being the "coolest" gifts we ever gave. Unexpected, and much appreciated by the recipients. Except maybe that one time when we were quite a bit older and she decided to do another round of model kits but this time, everyone could choose their own. One of the sons-in-law asked for a Ferrari, via a sister who heard Volare, and cool wasn't really the word he was looking for to describe what he got.

Our Mom was strong in the belief that perception is the source of most humor, and we kept proving her right. She was explaining to René, when René was young, definitions of "sexual": Hetero, Bi, Homo. René thought about what my Mom told her for a minute and then said, "Oh, okay. I understand now." And then, "There must be a lot of homosexuals in Tacoma." Our Mom, "Why's that?" René, "Because they even have their own special milk. You see the sign for it at the store all the time: Homo milk." The mystery of the signs, solved!

Lessons learned from our Mom: You can be right or you can be happy, or you can be both. And it doesn't even take a lot. Want a crystal ball that tells you the future? Get a snow globe of Tacoma with silver glitter so it's always raining; pick one with a pothole in the middle of the road and you've just raised your game from prediction to certainty. Want to prove that you didn't waste your money by investing in weather-changing technology? Buy a weather gourd in the desert then bring it back to Tacoma so that when you shake it and it rains you can go, "See! It worked!" Someone wants you to do a reading for them but they fear the Tarot? No problem, just ask them to get out their Old Maid deck and pick some cards, "Your future career will involve---wait for it---putting out fires like Billy Blaze! On your next vacation you will be singing like Alto Annie. Your love life? Greenthumb Gert says someone will be bringing you flowers." Because really, it's so much easier to be happy when you're right.

———

Before our folks married, our Dad predicted that they'd have six daughters and our Mom said, "If you're so smart, why don't you name the girls and I'll name the boys?" And so it was that our Mom named all of our dogs. (Both sexes.) As it turned out, a very good deal for us kids, since though our Dad tended toward French names, our Mom's taste was a little broader. If you discount the first, Tammy, as she was adopted from an Air Force family being stationed overseas and already had a name, and note that in an odd coincidence our Mom named six dogs, we could have been: Clementine, Skimo, Sissy, Poopy-L, Lucky and Happy. (Happy was a Grand-pupper, but one our Mom named.) So yeah, we are perfectly fine with having won the Dad-naming lotto.

———

We all do have a special place in our hearts for dogs, and we do honor them, because it was dogs, after all, who made our lives easier. To Lucky the First (who was not so lucky) for being the pupper our Mom and Uncle, when they were young, practiced their dentistry on by pulling a tooth for the poor dear. Had it actually been the worst tooth (and not just the really bad one. He was a very old dog) the dog would've likely been more grateful. Because of that, we sit here now and can unequivocally say that every one of the teeth our Mom ever pulled (and she was happy to pull our loose teeth) was the right one. And then there's poor Tammy. She wasn't feeling so well once, so the vet told our Mom to take her temperature. What the vet didn't tell our Mom was to put Vaseline on the thermometer and wow, who knew a dog could fly across a garage so fast?! We were more than happy to have had our temps taken under the tongue or under the armpit. Thank you, Tammy!

Our Mom always told us she loved pulling teeth. She'd say that the crack/crunch sound they made when they came out was so satisfying. She'd look at a loose tooth and then give us a deadline to get the tooth out or she'd pull it herself. And if we didn't, she did. Imagine our surprise when she told us, as adults, that she really didn't love pulling teeth, she just knew a very loose one needed to come out before we went to sleep so there was no risk of us choking on it. We weren't nearly so surprised that those words were accompanied by a bit of a wicked smirk.

Because our folks lived in the other half of Roxanne and Marty's duplex, their dog Happy (named such by our Mom because she was such a Happy girl) was also a part of their daily lives. After dinner one night, Happy came into the house smelling to high heaven. (She must have been skunked thirty or forty times over the course of her life. The next-door neighbors used to feed them and therefore had a surfeit living under their shed.) Roxanne and Marty began preparing a bath and our Mom, who was lying on the floor, stretching, said to Happy (who did not love baths), "Grandma wouldn't do that to you. Grandma loves you no matter how you smell." Then Happy, overwhelmed with gratitude, dive-bombed her and put it to the test by trying to hide under her, causing our Mom to have to go take a bath of her own. And so it was that our Mom came to make a sign for Happy's doggy door---a skunk in a circle with a diagonal line through it---a reminder that skunks were not their bosom buddies.

———

Our folks 'grand-doggie, Happy, needed to go the vet and our Dad offered to take her. They got out of the car and were about halfway up the walkway when Happy melted into a boneless mass on the sidewalk. Our Dad stopped, looked at her, and said, "You can go in on your own four feet with some dignity or I can push you in on the toe of my left boot. Up to you." Since she was no dummy and knew her grandpa made no idle threats she decided to make it look good---tail high, it was my idea---when she got up and walked in on her own four feet.

———

Roxanne and Marty have commonly been asked how they've dealt with privacy issues, having our folks living in the other half of their duplex. Well, as it turns out, quite easily. Shortly after our folks moved in our Mom gifted them with a handmade door-handle sign that said, "Please Do Not Disturb. It's Playtime for Roxanne and Martin". Exactly what one might expect from a Mom who had written on her and our Dad's bedroom door, when we were all still at home, in VERY large permanent marker letters,

STOP!
LISTEN
KNOCK
LOOK
AT YOUR OWN RISK

Was our Mom ever insulted when, as adults, we told her that we always thought filet mignon was just any cut of beef with bacon wrapped around it. How we had totally failed to grasp that those meals were rare and special because of the steak was beyond her ken. Which we might actually feel bad about, if not for the fact that we each have a story about how we came to understand that filet mignon describes a specific cut of beef and not just any random steak with bacon wrapped around it, and every one of those stories involves being an adult who ordered or was offered filet mignon and wondered aloud about how it could be called filet mignon without the bacon wrap.

What they don't teach you in "home" economics. Desiree had a paper route when she was twelve or so, and we other sisters often helped out. She had individual arrangements with the older sisters, but when it was Suzanne and Roxanne helping, she carried the bags with the papers and they ran them up the sidewalks to the porches. For their efforts, they were given nickels and pennies since they did not yet understand that one could purchase nickel or penny candy with money other than pennies and nickels (they even thought all taxes had to be paid in pennies), and were therefore happy to get them, whether or not they represented the going rate. And since our Mom was so thrilled that Desiree was keeping them busy and wearing them out that she would have been happy to send them for free, she refrained from getting involved in any negotiations; though she did suggest, when work condition complaints became annoying, that they could unionize. (She was from Detroit, after all.) Our Mom enjoyed pointing out that Desiree spent her adult life in management, some of it in union negotiations, and the rest could take great pride in how well we trained her for that.

Our Mom always claimed that we all have strong traits we picked up from what was going on with her while she was pregnant with each of us (personality, focus, interests, lifestyle) and we'd be the last to argue with that conclusion. Pregnant with Desiree, she was business-driven and achievement-focused. She was in school on the first leg of what would ultimately be twenty years to earn her degree. Desiree earned her degree in a much more traditional time frame but did so in a very male-dominated field. And to this day, Desiree enjoys taking classes. Pregnant with Deanna, she was focused more inward, on family and hands-on figuring out of how household items worked, like appliances and such. Deanna has five children of her own, and made a career out of figuring out how mechanical systems work. Pregnant with René, she was focused on good and evil, right and wrong. René would be dunked in Lourde's because it was when our Mom was pregnant with her that she visited there. René is known for being black and white, with very little gray, in her thinking. Ethical matters are a priority to her, and she values adherence to them. Pregnant with Nannette, our Mom experienced the best and worst of times as she was having a most wonderful pregnancy; and then her Dad died. Thus, Nannette is our Mom's Dickens' child, who does nothing by half-measure. It's great or it sucks, not much in between. Pregnant with Suzanne, everything that could go right, did. Even things that went wrong, were right. Suzanne is her Midas Touch child, and we like to say that if you set Suzanne to digging shit in Alaska, she'd find a gold mine. She'd have worked hard for it, and she'd have found it. Pregnant with Roxanne, our Mom was contemplating man's inhumanity to man. Our Dad was gearing up for his first tour in Vietnam, America was in a time of deep conflict, and our Mom was focused on peace. Roxanne is her "Give me your tired, your sad, your hurting; but don't give me any of your shit" child. Roxanne is the philosopher, who has never had any tolerance for meanness. All of us are happy to say that we are who we are because of who our Mom was.

Nannette's nickname was "Homewrecker" as she was a very active child, always into everything. Our Mom liked to tell about how they put Nannette in a chicken-wired box in the yard when Nannette was a tot, to keep her contained, and she figured out how to unravel it. When the older sisters were young (Nannette is number four) our Mom volunteered at a Girl Scouts day camp they attended. Nannette came with her, and spent her time hanging out in the sandbox that was being utilized for accompanying kids. The people monitoring the sandbox set about identifying the kids there and that nickname gave them just a little bit of trouble because Nannette thought it was her name so her unwavering response to each different way they asked was, "My name is Homewrecker." Concerned that they wouldn't be able to track down the parent of a kid who maintained that her name was Homewrecker, the adults in charge of where Nannette was playing prevailed upon the military special services detail to help them figure out who she was. (The camp was on base and the refrain for solving problems on base is, "Need help, find a uniform.") They took her to their medic station and the medics were very relieved when our Mom showed up and identified her since she liked her name and didn't appreciate their efforts to convince her that she must have another one. She'll still answer to it, today; with a sly grin attached.

―――――

Our Mom was left-handed (and though all six of us are right-handed, we all do many of the tasks she taught us left-handed), so she thought it great that they were on the left-hand side of the mirror-image duplex they lived in after they retired because that made everything more accessible for a left-handed person. That also made it the unit on the left side when facing them from the street, so our Mom was happy that that'd be how she'd be able to describe their place when giving directions, since left is such an underused word in a right-hand world. That worked out so well that when they got the front doors painted a few years later, she had their door painted red; a visual clue for all the people she'd had to grab up in the driveway before they knocked on the wrong door and say, "Your other left" and then have to hear, "Oh, right."

———

Our Dad's rules to live by: 1. Always be able to look yourself in the mirror. (You know the right thing to do; do it.) 2. Never be embarrassed to hear your name called in a crowd. (Do not be ashamed of who you are, where you are, or what you are doing; or don't be that, be there, or do that. It took us a while to grasp that one since really, we weren't embarrassed to be at that party drinking and smoking weed with our name being yelled by friends from across the room. Nope, we were perfectly fine with it all until it was our folks calling our names and we were so totally busted. Proving that your too-cool-for-parents teen-aged self actually has them? Now that, that was embarrassing.) 3. Never say thank you for a paycheck. (Earn it.)

———

Our Mom would be the first to tell you that having kids turns you into a walking dictionary that is expected to explain everything; even when those kids are adults. Our Mom to Desiree, "Will you rub my back?" Desiree, "Which part?" Our Mom, "The shoulders---down to the waist. You know, the definition of back."

———

At seventeen years of age our Dad was a fresh-faced punk from the mean streets of Detroit, who'd never been anywhere near wild animals, heading to the Alaska wilderness: where uninvited guests had a whole different meaning. He was out on ski-patrol, five guys total, all of them tired from a long day and settling in for the night when: BEAR HEAD!! IN THE TENT! And that bear was looking at them like coming all the way in, having a little snack, and bedding down there for the winter would work out just fine for him--- Holy Mother of God. Five guys, five rifles, five rounds of ammunition issued; all of them to the patrol leader, and all of them in the patrol leader's rifle. Which he fired, five times. And missed, five times. At point-blank range. (That can happen when the rifle is pointed upward and therefore shooting holes in the roof.) The bear looked at them all like, "Damn! You people are UN-friendly; and skittish." Then the bear backed out, turned around, and left. Gone but not forgotten, as we slept in Army tents all our young years, whenever we went camping, with flaps our Dad made sure were fully secured.

And, here comes another from our Dad's annals of Military Misadventures. A GI he was and yet this is a sea story: In late July of 1956 our Dad was on a troop ship headed from Alaska to Tacoma. As he recalls it, they were just outside of Puget Sound, in a heavy fog, and had picked up the pilot to guide them in. He was on duty on the deck when he looked up and saw: TANKER! RIGHT ON TOP OF THEM! And nowhere to go. Not quite nineteen and he thought that oil tanker was the last thing he'd ever see, but the fates were conspiring in their favor: the tanker had just unloaded its oil and not taken on all its ballast, so it was riding high in the water and it hit them high on their ship. The tanker had seen them and was in full reverse when it hit, so not at full speed. It did, however, still do some damage. They were ordered to move a bunch of heavy stuff to the other side of the ship, which kept them afloat, and they were able to limp into Seattle, just a slight change of course from their Tacoma destination. Does our Dad see boating as a vacation option? Oh, hell no! Infantry all the way, our family vacations were out in the woods, hiking and camping.

Our folks took up backpacking, cross-country skiing and photography after all of us kids were grown. All those activities were so close to being in Alaska when our Dad was a young soldier that is it any wonder that they even ended up with a bear scratching its back on their tent post? Our Mom (urgently whispering), "What should we do?" Our Dad, "Shut the hell up!"

Our Mom had an emergency plan for pretty much everything so no one was surprised to hear that when our folks were at Glacier National Park, she purchased a walking stick with bells. We weren't even surprised to learn that when our Dad asked, "What did you buy that for? If you get between a Mama Bear and her cubs, bells aren't going to save you." our Mom replied, "That's why you're going to be the one walking in front."

Our Mom always loved photography but never had the funds for lots of film. That changed some after we all moved out and both of our folks really got into taking pictures when they were backpacking and cross-country skiing. (Some of our favorite photos are of our Mom taking a photo of our Dad and the scenery he was taking a photo of.) But you'd have to say, if push came to shove, that our Mom won the prize for greatest obsession. When they were backpacking along one mountainside our Dad went "swoosh!" (not having been pushed or shoved) and when our Mom looked over, she found he'd slid down the side of the mountain and landed in a ditch. Our Mom "Could you stay right like that for a second? Just until I can get my camera ready?"

———

"So, Mom, any idea who you are going to vote for?" Our Mom, "I don't discuss who I am voting for, even when I'm a campaign manager." Our Mom campaign-managed for a candidate for the state legislature when we were young. (She enjoyed the pomp and circumstance of political processes. The same things she loved about church---and Las Vegas.) We've had people ask us, over the years, why none of us are politically prone and we'd have to say that there's probably no one more less likely (See how we did that? More/less: double speak. Learned that back then) to wear a campaign button or put a sign in their yard than the school kids who were making the name recognition ones.

———

Our Mom wasn't much of one for banal social niceties. If you asked her a question, she'd give you an honest answer. And we were good with that, because it informed our next steps. If you asked our Mom, "How are you doing?" and she said, "I'm feeling talkative," you pulled up a chair. If you asked our Mom, "How are you doing?" and she said, "I'm feeling like a bitch", you knew right then that you'd be saying, "Oh, look at the time!"

———

Our Grandma wanted our Mom to succeed in school. She wanted her to have opportunities she had not had herself and since our Mom worked after school, she took as many household obstacles out of her path as she could. Our Mom never even had to stir her own coffee. So, when our folks married, our Mom didn't know the first thing about cooking. She told us she fed our Dad so many hot dogs in the early months of their marriage that she expected him to come home saying, "Hot Dogs! Hot Dogs! Get your Hot Dogs, here!" Cooking was something she would come to have fun with, if never love, and when microwave ovens came out, they joined her love of gadgets to having fun with food in a way that was great for us kids. For instance, Peeps. We spent hours, every Easter, putting Peeps on a plate and watching them grow to plump chickens in the microwave. (It only takes over-cooking those once, and having to clean out the microwave, to learn the proper "cook" time.) Bonus round? Take the Peep out, let it cool, pull it back and forth between your fingers for marshmallow taffy. But the ultimate? When our Mom figured out that if you put a hot dog in a bun, then rolled it inside a paper towel and zapped it, it made a perfect dog. And our Dad got to experience all the nostalgia of, "Hot Dogs! Hot Dogs! Get your Hot Dogs, here!"

———

Oh yeah, there is such a thing as an inherited pet peeve. Ours is nails. Our Mom was big on saying, "If you're over the age of twelve, your nail polish should not be chipped. And, your nails should be kept at a uniform length, though not too long a length because that suggest laziness since really, what are overly long fingernails good for besides picking your nose?" Her Ma was big on saying, about some of the wealthy kids our not-wealthy Mom went to high school with who had raggedy nails, "Proof positive that money doesn't buy class." So there you have it; we may not have been rich, but our nails had class.

———

"At any gathering, only eat food out of the same dishes as the food being consumed by those who prepared the dishes." (This Public Service Announcement brought to you by our Mom; after she learned that Desiree marked the brownie pan the fly didn't fall into and die for select consumers [thankfully for her, our Mom included] while the pan the fly did fall into and die was given to the little guys.)

———

Some kids, complaining about how, "My parents won't buy me this, my parents won't buy me that." Our message to them is, "Suck it up! Hell, our Mom wouldn't give us 50 bucks to get out of jail; and that was in Monopoly." (She was a brutally competitive game player. Let you win because you're a kid? Pshaw!! Learn to earn!)

———

Never underestimate the value of a good slogan! When we realized that there were food items we could get from the commissary that weren't available at the grocery store, our folks had to explain to us about regional markets and the like. In doing so, we learned about items that were only available where they were raised, and ones that had gone national. One of the national items was a beer that originated in their home town so we asked why they never drank that. Our Mom, "Because my Ma always said, 'Beer that shall remain nameless, here: a headache in every bottle.'" Their competitors would be thrilled to know that we compared notes and, even during the rebellious years, none of us ever cracked a beer with that label.

———

It was always a true education, asking our Mom's Ma about anything. "Grandma, why is there so much head-bowing in church?" Grandma, "Out of respect." Us, "Out of respect for what?" Grandma, "Out of respect for all the people who drank too much the night before and feel like their head is going to fall off."

———

We often called our folks The Ed and Ruth Show because of her humorous approach to things and his dry one but who would have guessed that a trip to the hospital would be such a perfect demonstration of that?
Fortunately, our Mom did not spend nearly the amount of time in emergency rooms that one might expect for someone who experienced young-onset Parkinson's

Disease and the accompanying loss of balance and freezing of gait. Difficult and halting speech are also hallmarks of Parkinson's Disease, and our Mom became very slow-speaking and low-voiced. Add to that the "facial mask" that conveys no emotion and hospital visits could get interesting.

Our Mom had a minor head injury from a fall and the emergency room doctor was trying to establish if she was confused and asked first for her birth date and year, and then Roxanne's. It took her a minute to answer for Roxanne's so the Doc said, "You are definitely confused." Roxanne asked, "Do you have six kids? I'm the youngest and she just did what parents do: ran through five other names and dates to get to mine. That takes a minute." (Every parent out there nodding in agreement.) On a (years later) trip to the emergency room she got quiet so Roxanne asked if she was okay and she said, "Yes, I'm just going down the birthdays to get yours set in my mind because I'm sure they'll be asking for it and you just had to be the youngest." (Every parent now nodding with empathy.) The Doc came in to speak with her after they did a CAT scan from which she returned saying, "That was just like Star Wars!" and did indeed ask for Roxanne's birthday and then asked our Mom who the President was. Our Mom, "Obi (pause) Wan". (It was during the Obama Administration.) The Doc, "You're confused." Roxanne, "No, she's funny."

When the CAT scan results came back it was determined by our folks 'small town triage hospital that flying her to another hospital was in her best interest, so Roxanne asked the helicopter paramedic if our Dad could accompany our Mom. He said (good-naturedly), "Sorry, not this time. You'll have to have your helicopter adventure in Vegas or something." Our Dad, "The only thing on the face of this earth that would get me on a helicopter is Ruth." Paramedic, "Not the adventurous type, huh?" Our Dad, "The last chopper I was in was being stitched by machine gun fire." Paramedic, " Okay, you win; more adventurous than I am," and earned the dry look from our Dad that we were used to seeing when we said something ignorant and had to concede the point.

It is an indisputable fact that our Dad is a curmudgeon. Though he's mellowed with age (kind of a reverse curmudgeonry), he can still very much be brusque, impatient and irritable and we would love for all the people who consider themselves fluent in sarcasm to experience the work of a master. As he ascribes his personality traits to his ethnicity, it tickles our Dad that when he once said to a doctor, "No, I'm not depressed," the doctor replied, "I agree. You're just more morose than most." (He's not really gloomy, he's just really dry. For instance, when asked by that same doctor what he was going to do about something, he said, "Since I've been statistically dead many times over for a lot of years, I'm going to worry about it as much as I would have had those actuaries been right.") He is also just a big old teddy bear with a soft heart who, the more concerned he gets that someone is hurting, the more abrupt he gets. So, how did we really know that our Mom was doing well while in the hospital? We asked him if he was still growling at the hospital staff and he told us that he'd toned it down to a polite growl...maybe what one would even call an affectionate growl.

———

As for the rest of us? Our Mom was a vibrant,

independent, strong-willed individual. She would go down fighting every time, and would not allow infirmity to get in the way of what she wanted to do, even when she was a bit unstable on her feet. So, her daughters as they heard the news of the fall that required hospitalization? (Roxanne, who was there, had already told her that she'd have bought her a Halloween mask, she didn't need to make one of her own.) One sister, "This isn't a holiday! When did we start pre-holiday falls?!" (Earlier falls, very minor, were on holiday breaks.) Next sister, "Looks like we need to get some heavy duty glue and glue her ass to a chair!" Another sister, "Time to invent one of those bungee cord thingies like they make for kids, reel her in!" Next sister, "Mom always wanted an adult version of a baby bouncer. Maybe now it's time to design her one, keep her occupied." Last sister, "Too bad those big hoop skirts went out of style. We could have put balancers on one!" Problem-solvers, much?

———

Our Mom was a true extrovert. She loved to jaw with other people and she would say that if jawing was an Olympic sport she'd have us all beat since unlike our mouths that are filled with silver, hers was filled with gold. (Gold fillings.)

———

At the height our Mom did laundry for eight people, at a time when there was no permanent press, which meant everything had to be ironed. She wasn't always able to immediately get to the ironing so she'd wash the clothes, add starch, roll them, seal them tightly in a bag, and then put them in the deep freeze. (We were the only family in the neighborhood that had a full freezer; at all times.) Then she'd take them out and iron them in huge batches. Sometimes there was such a long stretch between those huge batches that we all thought we had new clothes as they circulated down the hand-me-down line. Neighbors thought it was hilarious, and especially wondered what she did with the laundry when we moved. Did she put it on dry ice to get it to the next post?! Is it any wonder that when we reached the age of ten and obtained the privilege of our own Military ID cards that one of our accompanying responsibilities was doing our own laundry??

———

Can you really blame a Mom for doing an end-zone dance because they so successfully hid a teenager's Easter Basket that it took them hours to find it? (It was on a blade of the really high ceiling fan.) Well, the rest of us certainly didn't, but Suzanne? Maybe a little.

———

During one summer, when we were kids, our Dad started coming to the dinner table without a shirt on. That really bugged our Mom so she requested he not do so. Well, our Dad, he still forgot at times, so rather than risk it becoming a habit, our Mom came up with her own unique way of making her request memorable; she came to the table bare-chested. Remembered from then on out, oh yes he did.

———

Our Dad got all sorts of sympathy for being the only male in a household full of females but if you think about it, it was our Mom people really should have been feeling sorry for since she was the one living out the Mom's blessing/curse, after all. (May your children be just like you.) Our Mom couldn't stand fourteen-year-old girls. She figured having to deal with all of us at that age resolved not only a significant amount of her own karma, but other people's, too. (We're pretty sure she'd have considered it fair to describe us as demons, notwithstanding that she'd say, if anyone tried to scare the fear of hell into us, "You can be a real pain in the ass, but I know you'll grow out of it. And all the fires of hell will never touch you; not without taking me out first.") And you certainly won't find any of us arguing that she was wrong in that. We know what we were like. That's how we got into the habit of saying things like, "Do you remember this from the age of annoyance?" instead of, "Do you remember this from when I was fourteen?" Because just saying the words, "When I was fourteen" was enough to make her appeal to another Mom and start saying a Hail Mary.

Our Mom and Roxanne once took a Western States train trip together. When they boarded the L.A. leg, our Mom looked around to see which way the train would be heading so that they could get seats water side and maybe see some whales. Such a conundrum that other people started trying to figure it out, too; right up until Roxanne said, "Call me crazy, but I'm guessing the train will be going the same way the seats are facing." (It wasn't like it was a European train, where the seats faced both ways.) Then our Mom said, "You go to the back and I'll go to the front and we'll see if we can get two seats together." (We'll just give you a second to let you process how that sounds both right and wrong, all at the same time.) They did indeed find two seats together and had a great time, that could only have been made better by more window seats. They jockeyed over the window seat, with Roxanne wanting it to rest her head to nap, and our Mom wanting it to see the view. Roxanne gave way on that. (Mom, after all. And one who wasn't above playing the Mom card. And really, her shoulder worked as fine as it always had as a resting place.) So it was with some surprise, when Roxanne returned from getting snacks, that she saw our Mom in the aisle seat and accepted her unexpected and gracious offer of the window seat. Roxanne figured the guilty Mom gene had kicked in or something of the like, but whatever, she wasn't going to question her good fortune, so she retrieved her pillow and was thinking just how great it was going to be to prop it against the ledge and lay her head down when a mouse went scampering down the ledge. Roxanne turned to look at our Mom and our Mom's attempt at looking innocent failed so she had to fess up that yes, that mouse had come that way before, going the other direction, and she'd decided she'd rather not be right there if it came back. And the rest of the trip could only have been made better by more aisle seats.

———

One sure way to get our Dad all riled up? Express sympathy that his fifth child was a girl, not a boy. The doctor who attended Suzanne's birth made that mistake, and then had cause to be grateful for the years of military discipline that saved him from that Detroit street kid decking him. Never let it be said that a Punk is bad father material. (In the neighborhood our Dad was raised in, one was either a Punk or a Hood. Punks successfully avoided prison, Hoods did not.) Most especially don't ever suggest that he must have been disappointed that we were all girls; not unless you want the daughters of a Detroit street kid to contemplate decking you.

———

Our favorite "Don't sweat the small stuff" story our Mom would tell us to remind us to just chill. Our Mom's Uncle was a simple man who enjoyed simple things. He worked hard and enjoyed a beer of an evening. He had a barn up a short way from his house which he found to be a convenient place to store his cases of empty beer bottles: year...after year...after year. Then one day, a couple of enterprising young fellas came by his place and asked if they could take the bottles in for the cash on the barrel they'd bring from recycling. Permission was granted and they proceeded to empty the barn: case...by case...by case. They got down to the last few cases and, with a huge sigh, the barn went "whoosh", and collapsed in on itself. It was the "Kabaaam!!!" heard round the neighborhood. Seemed the beer crates had been propping up the barn more than the barn storing the beer cases. Did her Uncle fret about the loss of the barn? Well, no. Being a simple man who enjoyed simple pleasures, he just pulled up a chair, popped a beer and, enjoyed the new view. It wasn't like it was the kind of tragedy it would have been had the barn caved in on full bottles, now was it?

———

Our Mom was a morning person (who woke up Grumpy, otherwise known as our Dad, every day) and did to us what many a morning person Moms did on the weekends: sang, played loud music, vacuumed over our heads, banged pots and pans in the kitchen; whatever it took to get us all up and out of bed because, she'd say, she was lonely. So lonely that she'd be up with us just long enough for us not to be able to go back to sleep before she went back to bed to catch up on the sleep she lost because we were keeping her up so late on those weekend nights. Revenge of the Mom, much?

———

An interesting insight our Mom had that is fun to test on yourself and family: We always knew that the best time to approach our Mom about something we were hoping for a positive response to was early in the day; our Dad, after 10 a.m. (We literally said, "Don't bother trying to talk to Dad before 10 a.m. or Mom after 10 p.m.") We asked her about that once and she said she noticed, after the first few kids, that we all seemed to be most happily aligned with our birth time. Her birth time? 6 a.m. Our Dad's birth time? 10 a.m. And the theory held true for all of us.

———

How do you raise six kids on an enlisted military wage with no outside help? STICK TO THE BUDGET! And that never varied. Years later our Dad budgeted a certain amount for books each month and was able to buy all but one in a series even though, with tax, the remaining book was $3.20. It would have put him $2.05 over the budget he set, so a no-go until the next month. (He could afford it, and he's not cheap, he just would not go over budget.) Fortunately, René was planning to borrow the series when he was done so as not to go over her budget and she bought it for him, whilst staying within her budget. And oddly enough, that actually put both of their books in the read for the month. (Sorry, not sorry. Just had to go there.)

———

Our addition to the realtor "location, location, location" list? A neighbor who overshoots their yard when watering. Mapped out by our Mom based on how the neighbor's sprinklers hit their yard, our folks 'place has the prettiest little summer garden; watered everyday at no cost to them. No small deal in the desert, where water doesn't fall freely from the sky like it does in the Pacific Northwest. And a great conversation piece, even if your answer to the question, from that neighbor, about how you manage to have such a lovely garden starts with the word, "Uh..."

———

Our Mom would settle disputes, like who had to clean what, in pretty random ways sometimes; like the time she determined Roxanne had to clean the floor because she was closest to it (shortest in the family) and Suzanne had to clean the ceiling and cupboard tops because she was closest to them (tallest of the daughters). And arguing that being the shortest doesn't stop you having to bend down or being the tallest doesn't negate the stepstool would only get you an offer to find something within easy reach to add to your list, which the middle heights were certainly happy to help her identify for you.

It's not unusual for us to have people tell us that we have odd perspectives on things. What can we say? We come by it honestly. Our Mom's Ma would say, "When right-side up isn't working out how you'd like it to, go upside down." She had her own way of actualizing an attitude adjustment: she'd lift her skirt (we never once in our lives saw her in pants), bend over, and look out at the world from between her legs. Worked every time! Like many Depression-era Catholics, our Grandma was accustomed to sacrifice and tight budgets, but she found a way to work with that. She and her husband asked our Mom to drive them to Florida once and, refusing our Mom's offer to help finance the trip, they told her they'd just have to skip a few things, budget a bit. Our Mom showed up to take them, during Lent, and found her Ma eating candy. Our Mom, "I thought you were giving up candy for Lent?" Her Ma, "I said I wouldn't BUY candy during Lent, I did not say I wouldn't eat it." (Sacrifice, made!) They hit the road heading south and our Grandma made our Mom refill the gas tank every time it got close to half a tank. Our Mom, "We've got plenty of gas, we don't need to stop for quite a while." Her Ma,

"It costs less to refill the tank if you fill it before it goes below half." (Budget, kept!) She definitely knew how to turn her own frown upside down.

Our Mom would always say to us, when we objected to something she said, "It's not what I say, it's what you choose to hear." And it's not as if we could accuse her of not setting an example for how that works. She was asked at a job interview, "Do you have any experience with blueprints?" and she answered, "Absolutely! I've dealt with them many times." And she saw no need whatsoever to point out that they were fingerprints---on the wall---in blueberry juice.

All in all, we can't say that a skewed perspective is the worst possible inheritance. We had occasion, when we were small, to ask our Mom what an inheritance is and she said, "In your case it means being grateful that you can't inherit debt." So yeah, though it was a long time before we understood why people considered it a good thing when they talked about their inheritances, we did come around to appreciating ours.

When our folks 'grandkids were young a number of them spent a summer at the duplex Roxanne and Marty shared with them. For some unremembered reason, our Mom wanted a hole dug in the backyard and though Happy (the dog) was more than willing, the rest could not be assumed to be, so she told the kids that she read in the paper a while back that Santiago's Treasure was reputed to have been buried in town and that if they found it, she'd split it with them. Excited as all get out, the kids were ready to randomly dig up the whole yard but Marty offered his services as a diviner to save them some labor and got out the dowsing rods and started a grid on the yard. That witching wand hit a certain spot and started quivering like a puppy at the door when it hears your car. Down, down, down it went---like a big fist of gold was drawing it in, and down they happily dug, certain that the gold was just a few shovelfuls away. The kids had an early-to-bed adventure, Happy found one of her bones (leave it to a pupper to make sure there's always treasure) and our Mom got her hole dug. Though in hindsight, it wasn't quite as well thought out as it might have been since she did forget to charge the kids for the privilege of digging in our yard for the treasure, thus adding some legitimacy like all those mining places do, so the experience was not quite all it could have been.

Daughters and spouses once took a trip to Lake Tahoe, where we stayed in a private family home. Our Dad wasn't able to come on the trip so our Mom was flying solo. There weren't enough bedrooms for everyone and rather than take one for herself, she said she wanted to sleep on the balcony and enjoy the mountain air. That lasted until she heard noises around her and was convinced it was a bear. Our Mom, "I know I've been sleeping with a grumbly bear my whole adult life but this is different." She then tried sleeping on the couch but there was a big wall of windows and she felt sure she was being watched: by a serial killer. (It's a Washington state thing, since it seems like the state breeds them.) Being the good children we are, we told her it was too late for cookies, but we made sure she had a drink of water, checked in the closet for the bogeyman and under the bed for monsters, then tucked her up in a spare twin bed in one of the couples 'rooms.

Those times when our Mom's sense of humor saved someone else's behind: Roxanne was late for work (she was a sole proprietor for a downtown retail shop) a number of days in a row because our Mom was doing a drug regimen change (common for people who have Parkinson's Disease) that was adversely affecting her stability. When Roxanne got downtown, she was being snarked at for being late by someone who had no vested interest in her schedule and who just couldn't hear that she would be on time unless she couldn't be. Roxanne said to our Mom on one of those mornings, "Person has something to say about my lateness, I'm going to lose my shit all over them and introduce them to the difficulties in moving when your ass has been kicked." She then left to gather her things and when she went to say good bye to our folks, our Mom handed her a note. It was literal. They had been in a situation where our Mom could not let go of Roxanne without the risk of a bad fall. And, it was just the chuckle Roxanne needed.
"Dear Name Withheld.
Please excuse Roxanne for her tardiness. Her Mother just couldn't let her go.

Thank you,
Mom"

The Four Corners Monument that marks the intersection of CO, UT, AZ and NM is a popular tourist stop. People commonly sit for photos on the round metal piece in the middle and put one arm and one leg in each state, but not our Mom. She crouched with one knee in the circle and the attached foot in a state, the other foot flat in another state, hands in the remaining states, and then said, "I'm not sitting down and proving that my ass is big enough to occupy four states at once."

After our Dad trained troops as a Drill Sergeant (and before he deployed to Vietnam) he was a Battalion Operations Sergeant. In that capacity he designed an Individual Tactical Training Course (ITT Course). Its purpose was to teach troops the individual maneuvers required in a combat zone. He was issued a certificate for that work that is a source of some amusement for all of us because with it came remarks about his "warm and pleasing personality". Our Dad, "There's not a recruit out there who would have signed that card, had there been a card." We think that someone out there had a sense of humor, added a little tongue-in-cheek, but we also like to think that someone actually saw that, under all his gruffness, he does indeed have a warm and pleasing personality.

You can see in the truly exceptional black-and-white photos of our folks 'wedding day that our Mom was absolutely glowing. In "polite" company she'd say she was so excited to get married and start the family she'd always wanted. To the rest of us she'd say, "My sex drive was greater than my educational drive and I was Catholic so…" (With many credits accumulated along the way, she completed her Bachelor of Arts Degree in 1980, at the age of forty, after firmly establishing the family she always wanted.)

―――――

Once us kids had all left home our Mom had a recurring dream where all her chicks were jumping out of her basket and she was frantically trying to put them back in. No need for Freud to interpret that one, not even the part where six daughters showed up as chicks. Though we did have to point out that, in our case, it had worked out well to put all her eggs in one basket. (How were we supposed to resist that one?!)

―――――

Our Mom always told us, "Marry someone who knows when to say no to you and will stick with it." Which is why it so amused us, as adults, when our Dad actually did say no to her (not something he did often, but she did come up with some things she wanted to do that someone with Parkinson's Disease just really could not) and then he'd come get one of us and say, "Your Mom wants to complain about me to you." We'd head on over there so that our Mom could vent. (All around the table together: daughter(s), Mom and Dad, while our Mom aired her grievances.) Us, "You know that thing you always told us about marrying someone who knows when to say no...?" Our Mom, "I never said you had to like it, even if he's right."

───────

Nannette to our Mom after watching her dance, "Mom, you have no rhythm." Our Mom, "Consider yourself lucky I don't or you probably wouldn't be here." (The Catholic rhythm method; a huge prophylactic fail.)

───────

When Roxanne and Marty were dating, our Mom asked Marty about his future plans. Marty told her that he aspires to retire as a Japanese snow monkey and since he was born in Japan (a Marine Corps brat), likes hot tubs, has monkey toes, and is a natural-born nit-picker (not that Roxanne has nits, but that he's prone to grooming stray hairs and the like off her clothing) he thought it doable. Always one to support people in their life goals, she gave him a branch and some bananas for his next birthday.

───────

Our Mom was always totally unclear as to why it is always artists, and not lawyers, who get the "My four-year-old could have done that." Because, really, who's better at technicalities than kids? Take Nannette, for instance. Asked by our Mom if she ate all the Flintstone vitamins she said, "No." Our Mom, "If you did not eat all the Flintstone vitamins, why is your mouth multi-colored?" Nannette, "I did not eat all the vitamins. There are three left. You can check." Nannette, who finally fessed up, as an adult, to being the one who stuck her finger in all the assorted chocolate candies to check the flavors and then inarguably pointed out that she was actually being thoughtful because it revealed the flavors to the rest of us, too, and eating a piece she'd stuck her clean finger in was better than one she'd taken a bite out of. She was also the one who memorized which chocolates were behind which windows in the cardboard Advent Calendar family friends gifted us every year so that she could get the biggest of the tiny figures. With six kids, four pieces each, dispensed at one a day, she had to will us to not pick the ones she'd already chosen. We didn't have a name for it until 1977 when we went to a round theater and watched that Imperial Starship travel overhead; however, she swears by the effectiveness of her Jedi mind tricks. Another technicality, since the rest of us are pretty sure that's a Dark Lord maneuver.

———

When we were tiny tots and would be sent to our room for something we'd done and were wailing at the top of our lungs about the injustice of it all, our Mom would yell back, "Louder, I can't hear you!" And we'd get louder and louder until we cried ourselves to sleep. Who could have guessed that our Dad's hearing would degrade so badly that, "Louder, I can't hear you" would become a lifelong refrain? Huh.

———

There was a drive-in movie theater within walking distance of our house in S. Tacoma. Deanna worked there as a teen. Before that time, though, we didn't know that there were shifts that only adults could work and our Mom was very happy to see that they were advertising a really good deal on Alice in Wonderland. The more people who came together, the cheaper the tickets. So, with some relief for a few hours away from kids, she sent us all off to the movie; the X-rated movie. That would be the last time she relied on a title and failed to check the rating line in the paper, by golly.

———

A downtown department store in Tacoma offered "Charm School" classes when we were teens. Our Mom thought it great; we could go there and learn a little about deportment and proper dress and the like, as she was definitely not fond of the trend toward heavy make-up and overdone hair. She, who rarely wore other than lipstick, thought it made everyone look like a street walker, and wanted us to learn about how less is more. Not as excited about the whole concept as our Mom but stuck because our Mom felt guilty that they didn't get to do all the same kinds of activities as older siblings because the budget was tighter when they came along, Suzanne and Roxanne went in the early '80s. It was four separate classes for which they had to bus to the downtown business district after school, and then bus home. Make-up day came and they were taught day, evening, and theater techniques. (The theater part we can only guess was added in case we ever got into beauty contests, like the person teaching it: Miss Runner-up Tacoma.) Suzanne was the model for that one and we don't know about runway walking but she definitely had a potential career walking the streets if the men who approached her at the bus stop on the way home were any indication. (And how happy was Roxanne that she'd removed her own name tag?!) Point made, if not quite the way our Mom intended to make it.

———

Ach, the ubiquitous school guinea pigs and hamsters. We know our Mom had to have greeted the news that one of us had the privilege of bringing them home for the holidays by thinking, "Shall yet another little soul be sacrificed on the altar of the Lord household?" How could she have not, since it seemed that someone in our family was always setting the poor caged animal free; free from its mortal body. (Not serial killer and small animals free; running around the house and accidentally smooshed free. We're pretty sure that explains why large animals have been overwhelmingly favored, across the board, by adult Lord people.) You know it's bad when you go to the pet shop and the owner just looks at you and says, "Again? What does it need to look like to fool the class this time?"

———

When our Dad was deployed on his second tour in Vietnam our Mom and one of her friends got the bright idea to do some ear piercings; then worked up the nerve to follow through by downing a pitcher of margaritas. Neither our Mom nor her friend had the first clue how to pierce ears but they were game. Our Mom went first, and forever after had holes in her ears that were more than just a little off-kilter with regard to her lobes, and each other. Then each of us was asked, in turn, if we'd like our ears pierced as well. Not having obtained any courage from a bottle and a bit intimidated by the blood, we all said yes anyway, and we each have ear holes that show a progressive level of competence as they went along; the little guys forever after grateful that seniority played. Our Mom's friend, meant to be last? Chickened out. And no, we never let her forget it.

Six kids later our Mom never could put on a diaper that didn't fall off. Even the plastic diaper covers weren't enough to secure them. And to lots of folks, that'd demonstrate she wasn't proficient in diapering. To our Mom, it was just great that any weight would drag them down and thus our diapers were self-removing when they needed to be changed. Stuck by diaper pins when we were little? Never! Having to have them pulled back up whenever we bent over? Always.

Can you accuse a kid of being the one who put frogs in the cupboards and other people's beds when all they actually did was capture a bunch of them and put them in the kiddie pool in the back yard and the frogs did the rest themselves? We're not sure, but we do know that there is some kind of confluence in it being the same kid who, as a toddler, customarily raised our Mom's eyelids when she was sleeping to ask if she was awake since having a frog pop out of the cupboard surely made our Mom's eyes go wide right before we all heard from her, with an, ahem, frog in her throat, "DEANNA LYNNE LORD!!!!"

We loved Peter and the Wolf when we were kids. We'd dress up in the old clothes and wigs our Mom kept around for that purpose and act out all the parts. Nannette loved the acting so much that she decided to ad-lib once and borrowed our Mom's black fake fur coat to became a bear and then stalked into the kitchen to catch René unaware. For a family that commonly doctored lyrics it's a head-scratcher that we never thought to doctor instrumentals; however, if only the composer had heard the ensuing cacophony, he would have had to agree that the entire symphony would have been enhanced by filling in the brass section with a trombone to match Nannette's stalking, a trumpet to emulate Ren'és reaction, and definitely a tuba to capture our Mom's response.

———

We were not a spider-friendly family. We had huge wood spiders that would come into the condo and it was always a debate about who would have to get rid of it. Never mind a phase we went through where we were sure we'd wake up one morning to a spider's revenge where all the floors, walls and ceilings would be covered in them; those spiders could jump, so trying to catch and release them never ended well for us and that meant their presence in our house never ended well for them. We were required to dispose of them ourselves unless they were too high up for us to reach, then our Dad would. Unintended though it was, that was just an invitation for us to bang on the wall under a low spider until it got too high for us to reach. (As adults, we came to feel bad about that after we heard the story about a spider that was so big that it audibly thumped when it dropped on our Dad when he was in the shower in Vietnam, which made it so he didn't like to deal with them, either. Not so bad that we'd have likely ceased doing that, mind you, but at least a little guilty.) Our Mom favored the vacuum cleaner until she had one crawl back out of the bagless canister vac. Then she started using large, heavy objects. Roxanne came to realize that change in strategy when she was a teen and came into the house from the deck and our Mom looked at her, picked up a big old coffee-table book, told her to stand still, then walked over and whacked her on the back with it. To Roxanne's outraged, "What???!!!" she said, "You had a spider on you, I had to kill it." Roxanne "Ewww! You couldn't have knocked it to the floor and then killed it?" "Oh, sorry, didn't think of that."

———

When we were kids and called each other names, our folks made us define the word we were using. If we could not do so adequately, they made us look it up. (Under the theory that you ought to know what it means when you call somebody something.) So just to be clear, if one of us ever calls you a name, we know exactly what we're talking about.

———

We didn't have a television through significant portions of our childhoods. For one period it was because our Mom tried to obtain a department store card to get one and the people there said, to her face, that since there was no guarantee our Dad would make it home from Vietnam to pay the debt, they wouldn't issue her a card. (Back then, it was virtually impossible for women to get independent cards. Needless to say, our folks did not further patronize that department store.) However, our Mom did enjoy the family interactions and creativity that accompanied the lack of a TV, so whenever we tried to become couch potatoes, she'd get rid of it. Not pull our TV privileges for a few days or a week; it would be locked up somewhere for months. So, it was with no small amount of amusement that we noted, once we all moved out, that our Mom ran a TV virtually all day long. She rarely sat down and watched it, she just missed the noise inherent to a large family. Not enough to regret the times she told us to go find something other than driving her batty to do, even if that something didn't involve a TV; but enough to offer to watch Sesame Street with us, if we wanted to catch up with what we'd missed.

———

We were a note-writing family. In fact, we had a notebook out at all times in which we recorded our requests of our folks, schedules, etc., dated and initialed by our folks, as it is not easy to keep the agendas of six kids straight. And, let's face it, we were not above capitalizing on the confusion to try and convince our folks that they had agreed to something which they had not. For instance, our Mom always answered no to anything we asked her when she was sleeping, thus we'd phrase things so a no was a yes. "Would you mind if…" The presence or absence of an entry in the notebook put a quick end to any debates on the subject. Once we were all grown and keeping track of our folks, the notebook went by the wayside, but we did have cause to wonder if it should be resurrected. Our folks took a much-anticipated road trip and while on it, they called Roxanne to tell her that they had gotten lost in the same place that she and Marty had earlier gotten lost that they had relentlessly teased them about. The only thing? Roxanne didn't even know they were on the road, and she lives next door. Our folks, "Oh we thought we told you. Huh, must have been your sisters. Don't you ever talk to your sisters?" Now, imagine how that would have gone over had we ever tried it. "I thought I told you. Huh, must have been my sister. Don't you ever talk to your daughters?" Uh-huh.

———

"Free to Be You and Me" is more than just a song that is a fond memory from our childhood, it's the general philosophy we were raised with. Our Mom did a broad range of religious studies and was looking into reincarnation at one point. She told us kids that maybe she was Joan of Arc in a past life. René loved that and couldn't wait to tell her friend, when he came to visit, the latest from our Mom. She told him, "My Mom was Noah's Ark in a past life!" The rest of us corrected her and said, "No, Mom was Joan of Arc. She couldn't be Noah's Ark, Noah's Ark was a ship." René, "If Mom wants to be a ship, she can be a ship!" And since ships are referred to in the female, like a person, who knows, maybe she was.

———

In the days before viral videos, when preserving your own dignity was tied to preserving the dignity of other people: Military people come from all over the place and their stuff travels all over the place, and it sometimes picks up unwelcome stowaways. When we lived on one of the military bases, we had cockroaches come up in the drain in the bathroom, so our Mom went to the neighbor's house to see if they were having a like problem. (It was a duplex.) Before she could raise the subject, the husband pulled their clock off the wall, shook the cockroaches out, and put it back. Realizing that the family was from a place where cockroaches were common and something that they had learned to tolerate, our Mom forewent speaking with them and instead conspired with base engineers to come do a routine check to make sure everything in the duplex was working properly (a common practice). At the check, they could note the bugs, order a fumigation, and supply information about what to do to keep them away in the future. All of which was done, without ever making the family feel as if they had done something wrong. As our Mom always taught us, and showed us by example, helping someone else be able to look themselves in the mirror is the surest route to being able to look yourself in your own.

―――――

When we were very young we slept on old Army cots. (Though never when camping. That was right on the floor of an old Army tent. We got a real chuckle once out of hearing a bunch of veterans complaining about the agonies of putting those cots together. We pointed out that Army brats often did the same but refrained from adding that we were all quick and efficient young experts at it, so as not to embarrass all the grown men whining about it.) Later, we slept on old Army bunk beds. When our Mom was a young mother, and still relatively new to Army culture, a veteran mom with a bunch of kids gave her a piece of advice she immediately put into practice, "Forget trying to deal with a bunch of bedding, just give each kid a sleeping bag. Same bag is then their camping gear. Saves on storage space, saves on shipping weight, easy to wash." Fast-forward to Roxanne in junior high school taking a Spanish test wherein she had to demonstrate that she understood the language to the degree that she could identify words she had never learned in Spanish by the surrounding context. Only problem? They used bedding for this test, and though she understood what they were seeking, she didn't have a context to answer in, having always slept in a sleeping bag. The teacher had to help her "cheat" by explaining common bedding items. This so amused our Mom that she went forth and purchased flannel top sheets (we did always have bottom sheets on our beds) and made Roxanne a duvet cover for her sleeping bag. Another bedding item not listed on the test, but commonly used in Germany where they were once stationed. Contrariness runs in our family.

Like many of our generation, we weren't really familiar with the concept of married couples having a "date night". Our folks went to the submarine races. And in our household, the yellow submarine won; every time.

We didn't eat dinner at our table, we dined on courses, just like wealthy people. Our courses being the result of different items getting done at different times is completely irrelevant, so just forget we mentioned it.

As if it wasn't enough that tiny tot Deanna once grabbed our Mom's faux pearl necklace and sent the beads scattering all over the church floor in the middle of a sermon (thank goodness it wasn't her rosary. Imagine how that would have gone over; poor Jesus on the cross being flung down by a Lord), she and Desiree were also the cause for establishing the church nuance involved in a penny being a penny, unless it's a coin. When they were small, our folks would give them a penny each to put in the collection basket at church. They could participate, and our folks didn't have to worry about them losing it. On one memorable Sunday, Desiree decided she'd help Deanna, and Deanna yelled, for all the church to hear, "But I want to put the penny in the basket!!" Forever after the money we were given to put in the basket was referred to as coins.

———

Yes indeed, our Mom brought fortune cookies to a potluck dinner at the Psychic Energy Center. And yes, of course, she put them in a pot. (Get it? Pot-luck. Some of you all need to work on your word play.)

———

People debate whether or not you can legitimately start a sentence with the word "and" (and yes, you can start a sentence with and) but rarely do you hear folks debate whether or not it always works in the middle of a list or the like. Most folks think it's pretty safe there, but Suzanne would differ. Our Mom used to leave notes on the fridge telling us what was available for lunch. Then she came home one day and asked a very young Suzanne, "How was lunch?" Suzanne burst into tears and said, "I just don't like hot dogs and jelly." And had to rethink how she wrote them.

A department-store Santa once asked Desiree and Deanna why they didn't have a doll on their Christmas list and they said, "Why would we want a doll? Momma has a new baby every year." Fifty-three months our Mom was pregnant. More than four years. Makes her claim to an MS and MD perfectly legitimate. (Mother of Six, Mother of Daughters, don'tcha know?)

Nannette accompanied our Mom to one of her humor engagements when we were all young adults. She was really enjoying herself, hearing our Mom rat out all the other sisters for things they had done. Then our Mom started talking about daughters in general and how we all had PMS and Nannette was saying to herself, "What? I never had PMS. And where could she possibly be going with this, anyway?" And then our Mom clarified and said yes, all of her daughters had PMS: Pre-marital sex. And then Nannette was trying to shrink down under her seat; mortified---and guilty.

It's not really all that difficult to see how people's

vocations became their last names. (Ours being Lord must be one of the most obvious. Or is that an avocation?) One of our favorite examples of people identifying themselves by profession was when our Dad was in the doctor's office and the nurse said, "The doctor is in," so our Dad replied, "Okay. The CPA is here.'

We always had an artificial Christmas tree because of our Mom's allergies. For us, putting up the tree for St. Nicholas Day and taking down the tree on Three Kings Day was a huge production, so, after all of us kids moved out, our Mom just couldn't get the same joy out of decorating the tree every year. Hence, she started wrapping it, fully decorated, in cellophane. Then she couldn't get the same joy out of putting the tree up every year, so she never took it down. She instead changed the decorations to match every holiday (Valentine's Day, St. Patrick's Day, Fourth of July, Halloween, Thanksgiving, etc.) with stuffed animals smiling out at you the rest of the time. When our folks finally retired and moved out of our last family home, our Mom made each of us a wreath out of one of the branches from that tree. Then she could visit it whenever she visited us during the holidays.

Our Mom put quotes on our school lunch napkins. She'd let a quote book fall open and whatever she first read on the page is what it would be. Our teachers would even put those quotes on the chalkboard every day. However, don't mistake us and think that she made the sandwiches that went with the napkins. She did not. Once we reached an age where we could make our own, we did, because it is no exaggeration when she said every kid liked peanut butter and jelly but none of us liked it the same way. (There is no connoisseur pickier than a peanut-butter-and-jelly connoisseur: peanut butter on one half, jelly on the other. No, both on one half with peanut butter on the bottom and jelly on top. No, both on one half with jelly on the bottom and peanut butter on top. No, peanut butter on both sides with jelly in the middle. And on...and on. 'Fess up, you have the way you prefer it, too.) No win scenario for a lunch-maker unless we made our own, so food for the brain instead.

―――――

Yes indeed, our Mom did give us Wonder Bread wrappers to cover our shoes to keep our feet dry when we were out playing in the puddles. Lots of feet to cover, but then one day of lunches was pretty much one loaf of bread, so it all worked out. Our Mom was a trendsetter for sure; if not of the high fashion she tried to convince us those colorful booties would be. Instead, she was late Depression or early environmentalist: reduce the original contents, reuse the bag, recycle what worked for her as a kid.

―――――

Should you use treats in training? Do the recipients actually know the right thing to do, or are they just addicted to the goodies and using the most efficient means to get them? Well, Deanna might help answer those questions. When Deanna was in kindergarten (while our folks were stationed in Germany, so, a true kindergarten), the teachers gave the kids a piece of candy every time they fell off the slide, so Deanna managed to fall off the slide every day. A tiny tot who already understood the risk/reward equation and hence was quite competent on the slide when our Mom was in charge and there was no candy in the offing.

———

Before a big event our folks were to attend, our Mom bought herself a "day to evening" make-up mirror that had different light levels and magnifications. Even though none of us was old enough for make-up, we each got to check it out and see how everything worked. Roxanne was last and when she sat down to check out all the various settings, she left all the rest of us laughing ourselves silly after she told us, quite seriously, that she looked best in it on the night setting and from a distant magnification.

———

René, nicknamed Sergeant Fuss-Puss when she was young because she liked everything just-so, added the accent mark to her name right around her eighteenth birthday, the day irony entered in her life in the form of Uncle Sam coming after her for a failure to register for the draft and potentially join the ranks of all sorts of folks who are all about having everything just-so. She had to go down and prove that the common male spelling of her name didn't in fact make her a male. (She accented the fe part of female, so to speak, and forever after became René.) Second bit of irony? Though the accent mark is considered a way to feminize her name in America, it wouldn't be in most cultures that use it. Thankfully, since she was conceived in Germany but not born there (it was close. Due to a storm in Charleston our folks 'flight was delayed until the very last day they would allow our pregnant Mom to fly), she was safe from them trying to conscript her, too.

———

Fat Tuesday, from Americans who come from the French Catholic tradition (Mardi Gras: our Mom) and the Irish Catholic tradition (Shrove {confess} Tuesday: our Dad) Indulge like tomorrow is the onset of Lent. (Because it is.) Two of everything! We don't care if you call it a doughnut or a donut, we're all over that! Fat Twosday, after all. Then confess, confess, confess, "Oh my God! I just ate eight pancakes smothered in real maple syrup! Then I had chocolate crepes! Then I slathered an inch of peanut butter on a piece of toast!" Which explains how we came to call the day after, among other things, "Ugh Wednesday".

———

Our folks got a piece of mail from Gerber that said on it, "For your baby", so they gave it to Roxanne, nicknamed Roxy-baby. Roxanne was forty-five at the time but, hey, once your baby always your baby, right?

———

When you're the people adding an extension onto our folks 'place, you gotta be grateful for all that our folks lived through that gave them their particular brand of perspective and humor. They had an extension done that required a portion of their metal roof to come off. No one was particularly worried about it because the metal roof covered an older, but still solid, shingle roof. And under most circumstances, no problem; that would have been plenty to keep out the elements. But, just their luck, heavy wind and heavy rain arrived, right when it was most exposed. Enough to crack a seam somewhere and let water through our folks' light fixture. They woke in a wet bed that was just getting wetter. Our folks, "We always wondered what it felt like to sleep in a water bed. We were pretty sure it wouldn't be our thing, and we were right! Now that we do know, we'll be sleeping in the living room for a bit."

———

Our Mom couldn't keep a watch running. Her electrical system just fried them. (She had a drawer full of dead watches.) Nevertheless, she had a favorite that she decided to try to get fixed and she was thinking to herself when she brought it in that it'd be nice if watch repair shops had a loaner watch (like car places) because she needed a watch to use, so she gave them her watch and said, as if it was standard procedure, "I'll take the loaner watch" and they gave her one. Who knew?!

———

Much to our Mom's dismay, our Dad does believe in capital punishment: our Mom would run up the charge cards, he'd cut off her capital. Which, frankly, didn't make sense to her since before they married (but after she wrote the DoD and asked for military pay scales), they agreed that he'd make the money and she'd spend it and really, how was it her fault that she was better at her job?! No worries, though, they found a way to resolve it. When our Dad told our Mom they weren't living within their income, she got him a second job.

If ever you have doubted the power of wishes, we are here to reassure you. Our Mom always wanted to live near running water. She wished deeply for it, as she longed to be able to end a hectic day with that soothing sound. And eventually her wish was granted and she did live right by water; on a hill right next to a storm drain pipe.

We can all honestly say that at no time, ever, were any of us angry at our Mom. We might have thought we were angry at her and lobbed, "You, you, you" statements her way but she'd say, "This can't be about me, so what's really going on with you?" Because, truly, how could her lovable self have done anything to make you angry at her?! (We joke about that but it is a great gift, to be taught some self-reflection.)

Context, the crux of any conversation, and definitely important with the conversations overheard at our folks 'place. Our folks have always been very practical and matter-of-fact when talking about death. It's a reassurance to kids who have a Dad in a combat zone, and it has defined how we've talked about it all of our lives. Our folks have both had DNRs (Do Not Resuscitate orders) hanging on the bookcase in their living room ever since they reached the age that statistics put positive outcomes on the negative side of the equation. After our folks gave up driving, René picked them up to take them to her place for a month-long visit and was helping them pack. She said to our Dad, "Have you packed your DNRs?" Our Dad (very dryly), "Why? Do you have some reason to believe we're going to need them?" It's a good thing, to be able to laugh about the hard things.

We're both a pretty creative and pretty practical family, in a lot of different ways, which has often caused people to ask us why we think that is so. Our answers tend to be along the lines of, "Probably stuff most never really think about; like figuring out how to wake up our very hard-of-hearing Dad, without touching him, while bleeding all over the floor and sobbing so hard you can't speak, much less yell. (After Vietnam he worried he might accidentally cause one of us harm if we startled him while he was sleeping, so we didn't touch him to wake him.) Then he'd wake up to anything from the equivalent of a paper cut to something requiring stitches and say, 'Stop whining and settle down! Or, I'll cut it off at the wrist and you won't have to worry about it anymore.' And then we'd get all sorts of practical about it." (His go-to statement when we were overreacting, that we still use on each other to this day because it always makes us laugh.)

While our folks were dating and our Dad was stationed in Korea, our Mom wrote our Dad a "letter" that would go on to be photographed for the Stars and Stripes. She took a giant roll of newspaper printing paper and filled it with daily events, cartoons, pictures, jokes, articles. The 1957 version of today's social media. The pages you see on modern platforms look so like it that we've had to wonder if someone along the way stumbled on that Stars and Stripes photo.

We're sure there is probably something James Garner did that we didn't see, but it can't be much. Our folks met him when they were stationed in Germany, and liked him so much that he was forever after guaranteed an audience in our family. They'd have been in their early twenties, Desiree and Deanna too young to remember. They were at a picnic for military people and James Garner was in the area because he'd just purchased a car nearby. (As we understand it, he was in Germany because he'd just completed filming The Great Escape.) He saw the uniforms and the picnic from the street and decided to join in with the revelry. Our Mom loved cars, and he allowed her to spend some time perusing his. (Real wood in the interior!!) Thanks to him from our folks for a wonderful afternoon, and from the rest of us for many years of viewing pleasure.

When one sentence tilts everything you ever thought you knew about your world right on its axis. Our Mom, starting to tell Roxanne a story, "When I was bed-hopping before you were born." Roxanne, "Excuse me?!" And then Roxanne heard a piece of her birth story that she hadn't heretofore known. The part she did know: Our Mom was very pregnant with her when she and our Dad and all the older sisters moved from Fort Ord to Michigan to prepare for our Dad's first tour In Vietnam. (All sorts of things to get done, not the least of which was to buy a house since back then, they kicked you off base when someone deployed and finding a rental large enough for our family was a no-go. The apartment we lived in the second time he deployed was technically too small for our family but a kind manager rented to them, anyway.) Our Dad was being retread to a new MOS (Military Occupational Specialty) so he was at school in Virginia when our Mom went in for a regular check-up. Our Mom was Rh Negative Factor, on her sixth kid, and the doctor was concerned about how tired she was so he told her he was checking her in for a month of bed rest. (There would have been more of us if not for the RH Negative Factor. Our Mom loved being pregnant and she loved being a Mom but the doctors strongly discouraged any more kids.) The part Roxanne didn't know: Our Mom was the only person in the ward at the hospital and our Mom being our Mom, she started bed-hopping to find the best bed, with an eye to which ones she would move to when she got bored with whichever was the current one, seeing as how she was going to be there for a while. Her "a while" would end up being a matter of hours, as Roxanne made her appearance a month early. Which our Mom reminded her of on occasion, would tell her that she still owed her a month of rest and relaxation, and did so again as an aside when completing the story. And just like that, with those words, Roxanne's world returned to its proper place. And really, how could our folks have known that ten years after her birth, the Police would come out with a song that made Roxanne's name synonymous with bed-hopping?!

Okay, we admit it! We're of a generation where parents commonly used whiskey on our teething gums, gave us brandy-laced hot toddies when we were sick, allowed us the treat of doctoring up (with powdered milk and tons of sugar) and finishing off the quarter cup of coffee our Dad would leave in his mug when he left for work and (gasp!) if we got our Dad a beer from the fridge, we got to take the first sip. And we not only gave Santa beer for Christmas, we also gave beer to the trash collectors. Oh, and our parents told us to go play in the freeway and threatened to tie us with a rope to the car so we could run along outside it when were acting up inside it. (Or was that one just our Dad?) We were the psychic generation, told to get lost but be home before the street lights came on. And, oh yeah, we sniffed purple ink off the paper produced by the spirit duplicator (which seems a rather apt name, in hindsight) at school, too. ("You want me to hand out the papers, teacher? Don't mind if I do.") It was what it was, and what it was is happy memories for us.

Having practiced her not-so-naturally-gifted hair-cutting skills (and we have the pictures to prove it) on us daughters when we were young, our Mom eventually started cutting our Dad's hair.

Unfortunately, she couldn't use the technique she settled on when we were a little older and had long hair and were just looking for a trim. She would run a wide piece of tape along the bottom, check it with a level, and then cut it. (Tape held all the hair. No muss, no fuss. Brilliant.) Not doable for him because he had a much shorter cap of hair, but she managed. However, in time, the Parkinson's Disease tremors she experienced made continuing to cut his hair impossible. (Though they weren't at all yet present the one time she was cutting his hair and just could not get the scissors to close. She finally realized she was cutting his ear. Good thing they were dull scissors!!) So our folks set out to find a barber. Now, our Mom kept her hair short most of her life and was so impressed with the barber's scissor skills, she decided to climb into the chair after our Dad was done. (He also fit her rules for choosing a hair stylist: choose the one whose hair you like the least since chances are, they are the one who cut the hair for the one you like the most.) At first the barber thought she was just sitting there while our Dad was paying the bill but then she made it clear she wanted him to cut her hair, as well. He was a little disconcerted, said, "I've never cut a woman's hair before." (And he wasn't a young man.) Our Mom. "Do what you normally do except you can skip the white walls and hold the face shave until I'm a few years older."

Our folks went through a fitness phase wherein they woke all of us kids up every day before school and had us run around the elementary-school track with them. We totally didn't get it since we all had PE and the little guys had recess and the older kids had sports, but nevertheless, we did our daily run and then listened to our sneakers thump, thump, thump as the dryer was tumbling off the dew to get ready for school. Many years later we read a story about a young man whose Dad had done the same with him and he too didn't get it until one day he asked his Dad and his Dad told him that running had saved his life in Korea and so he wanted his kids to be able to run, too. We told that story to our folks and they said, "If you're waiting for another explanation, sorry to disappoint but we wanted to get into shape and needed some motivation and rousting you kids was our 'work-out date' way to make us do it."

We always thought it a funny story that our Dad was detained for impersonating a sergeant when he was a sergeant, but evidently looked too young to be one to the military police. He always said it wasn't the error that bothered him, it was that he had all his paperwork on him and they still wouldn't release him until a senior vouched for him. None of that mattered to us, we just enjoyed teasing him about looking like a criminal---until we got older and similar things started happening to some of us (always chosen to be searched at airports, followed through department stores, etc.)---and we realized there is apparently a "looks like a criminal" gene that is not only generational, but multi-generational. You can usually tell which ones got it because some in our family either love or don't mind getting their photo taken and others are of the "dislikes getting our picture taken because so many seem to think it should be a mug shot" contingent.

Our Mom loved both taking photos and having her photo taken and she was big on sending postcards so she thought, when Marty was in basic training, that she could take photos of Roxanne and send them as postcards. However, Roxanne doesn't so much love either taking photos or having her photo taken and wasn't fully on board with that plan. Undeterred, our Mom said that, one way or another, she'd get a postcard picture to send to Marty. And so she did; she found a postcard that had a pair of cuddling harbor seals on the front and she tagged the individual seals with their names. Then on the back side, "Hi Marty, When I was at Port Townsend today, I found this picture of Roxy and you. Was I surprised! Roxy keeps telling me there aren't many pictures of you two."

Challenge, met! And though you might think after all of her years of experience with our Mom that Roxanne would catch on more quickly, but nope. She was driving our Mom to distraction with her hovering after our Mom fell and hit her head from Parkinson's Disease-related instability. (Our Mom, "You know that saying, 'love someone from a distance?' I wish you'd do that for me right now. And not in the emotional sense, in the literal sense." So funny!) So, the next compromise: a rugby helmet to wear indoors while our Mom was healing and when she was particularly unstable. (Because the fall occurred while she was planting, she was already wearing a full-face bicycle helmet when pursuing her passion for flower gardening.) Roxanne thought it was inspired herself, but our Mom said she wasn't so sure. She said if Roxanne thought it so cute, she should take a picture of herself wearing it and share it on her social media. So, Roxanne did. Before posting it she showed our Mom the photo and asked what she thought and she said, "Oh, I always liked the idea of the helmet. I'll be able to do more with less worry. You just don't share enough pictures." Roxanne, "Dang it! You got me!"

Our Mom worked with Tacoma's Mayor on the proposed World's Fair that resulted in the Tacoma Dome. For her work, she was awarded a key to the city. She also accompanied the Mayor on a trip to China in an attempt to establish a sister city there. At the time they were there, so many had never before seen a non-Chinese individual that people would follow her around, try to touch her. They were treated very much as honored guests, and regaled with tons of alcohol. The Mayor of their proposed sister city was so impressed with our Mom's ability to hold her liquor that he told her she was welcome to come back any time. (He never caught on to the fact that though she could hold her liquor well, she really never was much of a drinker so after the first night, the plants edging the rooms around the dining tables all held her liquor well.) We all wanted to know how she managed to eat all of the food that was truly foreign to our notion of edible and she'd say she just never asked what it was and that worked out fine until she was offered the eye of a duck as a reflection of the esteem for which her hosts held her. She'd thought she'd just swallow it like a pill but her hosts were watching closely to see what she would do so, she bit in and chewed. She said though it didn't have a satisfying crunch, it did have a pop to it, followed by a warm gush of liquid. Then she'd offer to go to a Chinese Market and see if she could find some to make for us. Us (never mind that Nannette sucked snails out of their shells when she was a tiny tot or that older kids fed younger kids worms): "No, thanks. We're good!"

One of Suzanne's college degrees was in Chinese language and literature. She had classmates who were marrying and would be moving to Taiwan and was invited to the bridal shower, to be held on Mercer Island. (Read: ritzy.) Suzanne immediately sought the counsel of our Mom, given her experience of having traveled to China, to help her develop a Chinese-themed gift. Our Mom said, "I know exactly what to do. Let's go shopping!" And so they did, and bought out a Chinese sex shop. Suzanne was so excited to be bringing authentic naughty Chinese toys to this shower that she could hardly wait to get there. Once there, she could hardly wait to leave; having quickly realized (she's bright that way) that it was a kitchen and bath shower, and most of the attendees were elder relatives of the bride. Cringing a bit, after a failed attempt to sneak her gift back off the gift table, Suzanne watched as the bride opened the gift, pulled out a rather racy item with a very large, very graphic illustration of proper use on the package, and the room went silent. Now mortified, Suzanne saw the horrified bride's eyes cut over to her Grandma and as the bride started stammering, Suzanne started looking for a convenient hole to swallow her up. None being available, though desperately desired, she froze in place. Then Grandma spoke and said, "Let me get a closer look at that." Nothing left to lose at that point, Suzanne finally looked at the Grandma and was treated to a wink and a smile. We think our Mom and her Grandma would have gotten quite a kick out of each other.

———

It's really a shame that Deanna doesn't live in the desert since she has a unique appreciation for sand. As a tiny tot, one of her favorite things was to dip her ice cream cone into the sand before she ate it. No matter what our Mom tried to discourage the practice, Deanna always found a way. She liked it, and that was that. To this day she likes crunchy food and has said that if she dropped an ice cream cone in the sand she'd still eat it, and enjoy the grit and texture. Our Mom, "Just don't tell Ben and Jerry! Water is already expensive enough for us desert dwellers, we don't need to pay for sand, too!"

———

It was a joyous day in Nannette's young world when the sand finally showed up for the sandbox in the back yard. She had waited forever to be able to resume her favorite activity after one of the family's moves and was finding it difficult not to go right out there and play, even though it was too late in the day. Resigned to having to wait for the next day, Nannette then overheard the neighbor telling our Mom it was going to rain. That was too much for her to bear and so it was that our Mom found her in the dining room, surrounded by the sand she'd been lugging in with her pail so that rain need not interfere with her plans to play in it the next day. A bit of a conundrum for our Mom as she could hardly point out that sand is meant for the outside since she'd already created a slide for the stairs to the basement to keep everyone occupied inside on rainy days.

———

As far as we know, there are only about five photos of our Dad before he joined the Army. We have one from when he was fifteen and rode his balloon-tired bike (given to him for Christmas so that he'd have broader means to thereafter entirely earn his own way) with a buddy about fifteen miles round-trip to the old gravel pit on 15 mile road at which time he paid fifteen cents to swim in what the owner had converted into a swimming hole. One of the very few times a kid raised in a state replete with lakes ever got close enough to the water to immerse. (In fact, he couldn't swim when he joined the Army but had to traverse the length of a pool; which he accomplished by taking a very deep breath, using the weight of his pack to anchor him to the bottom, and walking across.) We have the photo courtesy of that buddy, a happy day in the midst of what was a rather grim childhood. (Our Mom, with all her joyousness, must have hit him like a bolt of happy lightning.) He has never much taken to being in the water himself; however, every one of us daughters learned to swim early and spent much of our childhoods in water, in part because of that day.

———

Our folks had a hard and fast rule for us when growing up, created because of the loss to our Dad of a favorite cousin to an inexperienced driver: we were not allowed to be a passenger in a car with anyone under twenty-one unless we had a driver's license or were accompanied by a sister who did. Non-negotiable. On the night of Roxanne and Marty's first date (she fifteen and he eighteen) our folks were meant to pick her up at work and then Marty would pick her up at home. Roxanne had explained to Marty that he'd have to have someone twenty-one with him or our folks would have to drive, so imagine her surprise when Marty showed up to pick her up at work that night. Seems our Mom called him (and reached him, before cell phones) and talked with him for awhile and then told him neither she or our Dad was able to go get Roxanne so asked if he would. (Roxanne to Marty, "No, I didn't make up that family rule just to screw with you.") When Roxanne asked our folks about it later ("Who are you and where're my hard-core parents?!"), our Mom said, "I talked with him." (Enough said for anyone who knew our Mom. She trusted her instincts.) "But, don't get any ideas. Picking you up was an exception, not a new rule." (Also totally our Mom.)

———

Priorities: People, pets, plants, paper. That's the list our Mom would tell us when we were young. Then one day, when their place was having an addition added, the port-a-potty prompted an addition of its own. Fits the alliteration nicely, and definitely a priority when no other are possibilities are present.

———

If our folks ever gave the impression that they'd heard it all, that's because they did. They came home early from a trip and found Suzanne, and a bunch of her friends, having the all-too-predictable party in the house. Never mind the alcohol bottles strewn all over the place, Suzanne managed to convince herself that she could convince them that what they were seeing was a Bible Study. (She evidently didn't realize that beer goggles are not transferable.) Our folks told her that if she'd learned enough from her "Bible Study" to turn water into wine, they'd give her a pardon on the restriction coming her way. Otherwise, praying for lenience wasn't going to get her there.

———

It's always an adventure for the daughters, flying into our folks 'small, rural retirement town. We have about a 50/50 chance of flights being delayed, diverted, or canceled unless you're flying in with a goat. Desiree did that once, she and the goat the only passengers. An award-winning expensive goat, thank goodness, since otherwise she was convinced the flight would have been canceled, she not having the same stature. So Desiree felt some relief that they'd be driving and not flying when she took our folks on a vacation; no delays or goats in the offing. And they were enjoying a very smooth trip home, right up until they got held up on the highway; by goats. As our Mom told the rest of us later, "Not just any kind of goats, either; lollygagging goats. Taking their own sweet time crossing the highway, moving at the speed of…" at which point she was interrupted so others could interject, "You and Desiree?" Who are both known for taking their own sweet time. And you thought road construction was bad. Pshaw!

―――――

A trait René and our Mom shared is a tendency to mispronounce words and unintentionally corrupt idioms in new and interesting ways like Renés classic, when she was trying to make a deal with our Mom. "You know, if you rub my back, I'll rub yours." And since our Mom always enjoyed a good back rub an agreement to make her half literal, in addition to the other items in the offer, sealed the deal.

―――――

Littering is for the birds? Not! We're pretty sure every small kid goes through a phase where getting trash to the garbage can seems like more effort than it's worth (at least we're pretty sure we all did) when hey, you can just drop the trash on the ground. (That's before you reach the age when you figure out that you can say to siblings, "Here, take this!" and they will instinctively reach out for the trash you shove in their hand; then be stuck with having to dispose of it themselves.) Our Mom really disliked litter, so she came up with her own solution to teaching kids to keep our world beautiful; by telling us about how birds do it. Our Mom, "You see that box on the telephone pole? (Transformers.) Those are trash receptacles for birds. If even birds can manage to get their trash into a trash can, so can you." Of course we believed her, why wouldn't we? Though when you get a few more years under your belt you do start to wonder why those fastidious birds don't also use toilets.

―――――

"Dial-A-Superintendent". Never heard of it? You would have, had you been active in the Tacoma Public School District in the mid-'70s. A suggestion of our Mom's that, with just a little persistence, went into action so that parents, teachers and students had a direct line to an answering machine wherein all messages recorded were sent to the Superintendent. Our Mom had a letter from the Superintendent from when she first suggested the idea. It says, in part, " I also wanted to tell you that your suggestion of 'Dial-A-Superintendent' was received by so-n-so who got a memo to so-n-so on Oct. 15 who got a memo to the Superintendent on Oct. 17, the same day your second letter arrived." (Yes, squeaky wheel…) It closes, "It was a pleasure to meet you at the Urban League workshop. I won't say 'stay in touch' because I know you will." Turns out the phone line was a success, with people appreciative of a way to communicate concerns that they didn't feel rose to the level of needing to have to make an appointment for or address at a school board meeting, and it ended up being the Superintendent who stayed in touch.

———

Our Mom did her best to go eco-friendly while on a budget on numerous occasions, some of which worked out better than others. One attempt was sponges soaked in liquid fabric softener for the dryer. They were meant to replace dryer sheets. And they might have even worked were it not so static-cling-creating dry in that desert known as Western Washington, right by Puget Sound, which caused every skirt we wore to look like electrified gauchos.

———

Apparently, there are now many no-sew options to hem your pants to different lengths for different shoes. What?! The duct tape our Mom urged the less naturally gifted sewers in our family to use so as not to mangle the material when she didn't have time to baste is not good enough for some folks?

Military folks will recognize this one. Every time we asked our Dad for clarification about some military family policy that didn't make sense to us he'd say to start with this phrase and take it from there. "Uncle Sam wants you! But if he'd wanted you to have a spouse and a family he'd have issued you one." Pretty much.

We were raised in the Pacific Northwest, so there were some things that were really new to us when our folks moved to the high desert: We'd never seen lightning with snow, we'd never seen a "dry rain" and we didn't know weather could be site-specific. Our Mom would send her young granddaughter to the front window to check the weather and after she reported on the weather from there, she'd then send her to the back window to do the same. Her granddaughter thought that a little odd but a few days in, she found it cloudy and raining in the front yard, with blue skies and sunshine in the back. Then she didn't have to be sent; she thought it so wild that she did it on her own. You don't wait ten minutes for the weather to change in the high desert; you walk a block.

The cynicism you learn from your own young kids. Roxanne is a very trusting person; until she's not. When she was in elementary school she had received the Almond Roca she was supposed to be selling for Bluebirds (elementary-aged Campfire Girls. Our Mom had been involved in Campfire Girls throughout her childhood), and put it in her locker, and then never saw it again. So, our Mom bought her a lock for the locker, which Roxanne brought home that weekend. Our Mom asked, "Is something wrong with it?" Roxanne, "No. But whoever stole the candy would probably steal it too, so never mind." Our Mom thought to try to convince her otherwise and then thought, "You know, she could be right."

When we were in the teens to twenties range of ages we found a photo of our folks, before they were married, where our Mom was sitting on our Dad's lap. We were completely scandalized, as our folks were insistent that we were not to sit on a man's lap unless we were married to him. (Notwithstanding that the photo was taken not too far out from their wedding.) Our Mom, "We didn't have any choice, my folks ' house was so small and there was no other seating." Since the house she was raised in was maybe 400 square feet that was probably true, but you'll forgive us a little skepticism since she had a bit of a smug smirk on her face when she said it.

Numbers defined a lot of things in our lives, even before our Dad became a CPA. We lived on a very tight budget even after our Dad retired from the military as he worked full-time and went to school full-time to earn his Bachelor's degree, in three years, and then his Master's. All while still managing to show up for our extracurricular activities, PTA, etc. Our folks always kept a budget book and once we had jobs, we were expected to, as well. Our Dad would tell us, "Know the difference between being poor and being broke. One you can fix with money management, the other you cannot." They had to be so creative about money that our Mom even used our bicycles as assets to get them over the amount they needed to secure a home loan. And their way of dealing with budgeting for us kids was to use our ages to guide almost everything we did. Whenever we went to the Puyallup fair (the state fair) as kids, our folks gave us half our age to spend there. (Kids all got free school tickets. And everyone in our generation picked a flag color to meet their folks at when it was time to leave. No cell phones, then.) Our allowance before we had our first jobs was our age plus a zero a month; calculated in pennies. If you were eleven, you got $1.10. (A large amount to us since all of our needs were met and it was just candy money, and the small grocer we went to still had penny candy in his shop.) For grapes or nuts you could eat your whole age. Those are the ones we figure there wasn't a lot of long-term thinking involved in since more than one kind of inflation came into play as we aged.

———

Our Mom came to school with each of us, spent the

entire day with us, one day a year. She also went to open house nights and parent-teacher conferences; however, she wanted to observe, for herself, what our day looked like. We enjoyed it when we were kids but were too cool to have parents when we were teens and we'd come up with all sorts of reasons that we'd die of embarrassment. So, she'd save our lives by letting us pick her clothes and telling us we could act like we didn't know her. (And we'd have been glad to do that; if we didn't all look enough like her to make that laughable.) What surprised her the most about the clothes we chose for her? They were suits, when she thought we'd go significantly more casual. Oh no, not us. If we had to have her with us for the day, we wanted our teachers to worry that she was there on some sort of official business.

———

Though she did most often do recommended medical procedures, our Mom was of the firm belief that if men were the ones being examined, many of the processes would be less painful. And she wasn't shy about making her viewpoint known. Our Mom's doctor, "And when can we arrange your mammogram for you?" Our Mom, "Right after you put your testicles in the machine."

———

A bachelor gift to one of the son-in-laws was a subscription to Playboy Magazine. We think his friend thought it would embarrass the bride-to-be but none of us has any issues with the nude female form. (Hello, we come from an overwhelmingly female household.) However, our Mom loved magazine articles and it was no problem to redirect the subscription to her, so they did. Not too long after she was diagnosed with Parkinson's Disease she cracked her newest magazine and found one of the first articles she would read on the subject. Yes, we found for you the person who actually did read the articles in Playboy. You can thank us for it later.

———

Awkward! This is what we got for saying things like we have no issues with the nude female form; for not demanding negatives; and everything we ever did over the years that embarrassed our Mom. (Never mind that she always said she loved to be embarrassed because she thought, "The warm-electric feeling that surges through my body is the next best thing to orgasm.") We were going through photos that had been scanned on a flash drive and came across the negatives of the photos our Mom took at our various weddings when we were changing into and out of wedding dresses and street clothes. (Click...click..click...what??!!) Since she'd given us the photos, we thought them gone from everywhere else. (And we have no idea why we thought that, since our Mom never threw out a picture or a negative, no matter how bad or indecipherable. Wishful thinking, at its finest.) Us, "Dad! Who all has a copy of this flash drive? It hasn't gone family-wide, has it?!" Our Dad, "Look at it this way, much more awkward for everyone else to see it than you." He had a point. And we're sure we can count on everyone else to delete them, right?! (They are actually very fine, very arty photos. Just not meant for public consumption.)

———

Nannette didn't really enjoy high school. She was bored, so she just skipped going to classes; often. She was getting away with it, too, until our Mom wrote her a note excusing her from school for a legitimate reason and the signature didn't match the many other notes they had on file. Our folks tried about every incentive they could think of to get her to show up but with limited success. Our Mom even tried grounding Suzanne in the hope that guilt would make Nannette show, but creative punishment involving peer pressure didn't get them anywhere, either. They then got a call from the administration telling them they needed to do something about Nannette's attendance, so they did; they made an appointment with the administrators and told them that, as taxpayers, they were not willing to keep paying for a student who was never there, so they wanted her expelled. That's when the administration decided they could be a little more proactive in making school a more challenging place for Nannette to be. And Nannette did indeed graduate, and all were pleased with themselves.

It's rather sad to us that many schools no longer have shop classes. How do people today identify the teenagers in the neighborhood if not by the routered signs saying, "The Whoever Family"? We don't know where they all went but for a number of years our folks put up a new "The Lord Family" sign regularly; their preference over having a bunch of them stuck to the house at the same time. The advantage for all the aprons from Home Ec? There were plenty of us to wear them.

In 1977 we set out for a little seventeen-mile stroll through the Cascade Mountains with our Dad. (Our Mom dropped us off on one end and picked us up on the other.) Our strongest shared memory of that day was stopping to eat lunch, in the rain, in the woods, while standing, because the lake we were shooting for just refused to materialize. We finished eating and set back out on the trail and hit that lake just over the next rise and it was, of course, bathed in sunshine. Mystic Lake. Uh-huh. We took another little break in the sun and then set back off on our trek, at which time we lost the trail (or maybe better said the trail lost us with an impassable obstruction) and our little stroll turned into a twenty-six-mile haul. The greatest individual memory from that day is Renés. We had to cross a tree over a rushing river (with just a rope overhead to hold on to) and she remembers how she just knew she couldn't make it across, but our Dad's particular brusque Drill Sergeant way got her there, and how proud of herself she was when she made it. The hike was an agony for our Dad close to the end as his feet had been frostbitten when he was a young man in the Army, so René took over the backpack, and we trooped on. We think it a testament to our Dad's ability to raise morale that the photos we have from near the end of that hike show us smiling with accomplishment.

Our Mom loved to sew (virtually all of our dressy clothes when we lived at home were sewn) and she taught all of us to sew, though some took to it more readily than others. She and Desiree would spend many a pleasant hour together sewing and because they wore the same size, and shared similar taste, they'd be sewing for themselves and each other.

Once they lived in different states and were no longer regularly sewing together, we can't think of a time that Desiree visited our folks that she didn't leave shy of some of her clothes. We don't think our Mom ever bought her own coats or shoes or the like. She'd say to Desiree, "I really like those shoes" and Desiree would be heading home on a flight without them. Our Mom considered it fair trade since someone once said to her, when Desiree was just starting out on her career, "Desiree has such good taste in clothes." And our Mom forewent pointing out that they were her clothes.

———

We are not at all exaggerating when we tell you that you'd walk into the library with our Mom, and she'd be looking for specific info, and she'd be looking through a shelf, and she would accidentally knock a book to the floor, and that book would open to just the page she needed. Or, she'd grab a microfiche and never have to scroll; the last person would have left it right where she needed it. It was so uncanny that librarians even took note and said that she ought to be a researcher. For ourselves, we were just glad our folks had a firm policy about respecting our privacy (what of it we had, considering how many of us there are), since there was no question that if she set herself to finding some kind of illicit item in our rooms, no matter how well we hid it, it would have made itself known to her.

———

Our Mom went completely gray, overnight, in her mid-twenties, when her Dad died. She dyed it off and on over the years (and claimed it got darker on its own after we all left home) but mostly she let it be, as it was a really beautiful silver before it went a really beautiful white. She used to tell us, "Just because my hair is gray does not mean my brains have leached out." No, but we're sure they wanted to after some of the things they had to process from us.

Our Mom had to work to keep at her preferred weight because she would eat when she was frustrated with any or all of us and with six of us, that wasn't exactly a rare event. She tried many different approaches to break the habit, but no joy. If she was irritated, she was eating. Then came a day when Deanna was being particularly annoying and she set out to deal with her mad by slicing open a loaf of french bread, slathering on some butter, and following that up with a nice thick layer of peanut butter. Just as she was getting ready to bite into it she looked at Deanna and had a flash of brilliance; give it to her and tell her to eat it. She wouldn't consume the calories, and Deanna would have to shut up to chew. Lucky Deanna, it was something she liked, too, and she was happy to get the special treat.

You think you have it bad with kids following you into the bathroom? Try six kids in a one-bathroom house. How happy was our Mom when they got a detachable shower head? Then when she wanted to hear her own thoughts while showering she could just spray us from over the curtain, encourage us to move along.

It was our Mom who told us, when cable TV came out, that cable makes it possible for the TV to watch you while you are watching it. Totally freaked us out. (Did you ever notice that CBS even has an eye for its symbol? We did.) So it was with some satisfaction on our part that we used a shared streaming account to go over one morning and ask them how they were enjoying the show they'd been watching every night. Our folks: "How did you know we're watching that?" Us, with sly smiles, "Because the TV is watching you while you're watching it."

———

We could always tell the difference between when something was out of whack enough to bug our Mom and when she thought it had gone way beyond by whether she commented, or questioned. For instance, saying, "The bathroom's a mess" meant what it sounds like, but, "Do you have a pair of rubber gloves?" meant, "This is disgusting, do something about it now." And then she'd say, "I'll just get out of your way so you can get something done." She was thoughtful that way.

———

Levitation 1...2...3...4! That's what you recite while you're clasping hands before you lift our Dad out of a chair, solely with eight index fingers; and it doesn't work if you don't say it. Ha! One of our Mom's "special friends" (spelt w-e-i-r-d-o by our Dad.) told her, when we were young, that you can lift a person just by four people clasping their own hands together, extending their combined index fingers, and lifting under the knees and armpits. And, you can. At our Dad's fiftieth birthday party we were at a restaurant talking about it and folks around us (we aren't really quiet people) started saying they didn't believe it so we showed 'em, the whole restaurant full of people. We hadn't done it ourselves since we were young but it still worked like a charm. And matched our Mom's refrain that there is no burden too great to bear, as long as it is a shared burden.

———

Joy in a bottle! For us, our Mom visiting her folks in Detroit meant Vernors Ginger Ale. Those three words are guaranteed to make us smile. She'd bring back a bottle (then later a can) each. A six-pack for a six pack. We'd see that green label and oh, the anticipation and excitement! You can buy it anywhere now but at the time it was such a lovely treat; our Mom sharing a childhood memory while creating ones for us. And if we fought over who got theirs first, we'd have to kiss and make up, so good thing it was Ginger Ale with its stomach-settling properties for when you want to puke.

———

Our Mom was never a heavy drinker as her grandfather owned a bar and she saw the damage alcohol abuse could cause; however, when she did drink, she could drink everyone under the table. (She liked to order a B-52 on occasion, just to watch people's eyebrows rise.) And every once in a great while (like when the six of us got on her last nerve) she'd say "I need a drink the size of my headache!" and she'd forgo the beer glass and with a wink and a smile, drink right from the pitcher.

———

People often asked our Mom the secret to the longevity of our folks' marriage and she'd say, "I married three men: a soldier, a CPA, and a cowboy. (They retired in farm and ranch country.) I was just lucky enough that they all came in one package."

———

We all had to learn to sound like Star Trek's Borg, before the Borg, and describe ourselves as whatever our birth order number was plus "of six" since, for some unknown reason, telling people you have five sisters makes them think there are five of you and saying to people, "I'm not my own sister" tends to get a blank look in return. (Six of six even has her own patter about sixth-child syndrome since if there are only five, she ceases to exist.) So, for our folks' twenty-fifth wedding anniversary they had baseball shirts made up. All had our names on the front. Theirs had 25 on the back and ours had our birth number on the back: a nod to all the people over the years who tried to get us straight; and a hint for all the people who couldn't count. The only one with any kids at that time was Deanna so they were 2A, 2B, 2C. Maybe the only time in the history of our family where everyone present got it right.

———

Our folks were married in the Catholic Church in 1958 and had to undergo pre-marriage counseling by a priest. The priest insisted that the marriage was 51 percent to the male, 49 percent to the female; which our Dad vociferously objected to. As he told the priest, "We're looking for a partnership, a full partnership," On the brink of their wedding they were facing a circumstance where the priest wouldn't perform the ceremony, so our Mom said to our Dad, "Let it go. We'll live our own life our own way." At the ceremony, our Mom said her vows loud and proud. "I promise to love, honor, and obey", and then she turned to our Dad and said for his ears only, "Except obey." They told this story at their fiftieth wedding anniversary and were happy to reassure everyone that they kept all their vows, especially the "Except obey" part.

Our Mom always told us she wasn't from this planet. The evidence was pretty overwhelmingly in her favor from how she was a blue baby born at home in a blizzard (the alliteration alone is out of this world), to how she was allergic to quite a lot on the planet, to how she couldn't keep a watch running. And she certainly had magical ways like convincing Santie Claus not once, but twice, to postpone his stop at our house for a few months until our Dad got home from Vietnam so we could celebrate with him. We kids thought, "Look at how powerful Mom is! She even got Santie to rearrange his schedule just for us." We believed that she was not of this world, so much so that we brought her to show-and-tell so everyone could meet our amazing extraterrestrial Mom. And why not? Since she chose it. We never got away with saying, "I didn't ask to be born!" Our Mom would say, "You not only asked to be born, you chose me as your mother." We're good with that. Indeed, as we often told her, "Look what smart little alien progeny newbies we were, that we picked you."

As we're sure you understand, we took a hard hit when our Mom died, and we miss her very much. However, she softened the blow in so many ways: the first by always teaching us that beauty is found where you look for it. Our Mom died in a recliner in the living room. There was music and talking; all the commotion she always loved. Our Dad had been sitting in a chair next to her, holding her hand, as was their custom. Our Mom was fussy about her hair, which had been recently brushed by Nannette and looked great. (You know you just smiled to hear that.) Her feet were in socks that were favorites that Deanna put on her. (Anyone who ever saw our Mom knows how much she loved her cool and funky socks.) She was wearing a beautiful night shirt Suzanne had given her for Christmas and snugged into pillows René researched for best comfort. Her nails were festive from a trip to the nail salon with Desiree and Nannette, and she was under an afghan Roxanne had crocheted for her. When her breathing slowed, we thought she was just falling asleep. No panic, for her or us. Marty, who had been at work, was suddenly where he needed to be when he needed to be there to notify family. It was as if she had planned every detail in such a way that we could most easily accept that which we had not foreseen. It was, in fact, beautiful.

Our Mom also relieved any worries we might have had about the decisions made in a letter she wrote to the family a number of years earlier. It said, in part, "I want to assure you that any action you take on my behalf will be as I would wish it and therefore not something you need to feel guilty about. As you are all aware I need control of my own life above all else. It is imperative to me that you understand that my destiny is not to be relinquished to the medical community for any reason." After all the emergency services left, our Dad was going into his office to get our Mom's letter to all of us to reassure himself that he had made the right moves. (We had not been on a death watch and were not expecting her to die that day, so decisions were made quickly.) When he went by the bookcase our Mom's DNR was on, it floated off the side (that it had been firmly attached to for years, and had never fallen off of, before) and landed at his feet. We said to our Dad, "We're thinkin' Mom just gave you her last word on that." Love always finds a way to comfort. And finally, in her letter our Mom had the last word on our behavior, as Moms are prone to do, "Above all consider it forbidden to be maudlin."

Our Mom remains a strong presence in all of our lives, maybe best exemplified by a moment René experienced when staying at our folks 'place. She had a pain that ran from her neck down her back. She was standing in the bathroom, doing her hair, when she felt a healing touch on her back, just like our Mom's healing hands always felt. (Our Mom drew down pain with loving energy.) It so startled her that she turned to look for who might be there. (And then realized she had been looking in a mirror so no one could have been unseen behind her.) It doesn't much matter what you believe about how things like that happen, does it, when what you are left with is a warm glow? Love always finds a way to comfort.

It has been our pleasure to share these stories. Spending time with our Mom, the heart of our family, has always been to feel special, even if you are one of many; to see life as a grand adventure, especially the things that do not go as planned; to understand that there is more than one way to look at a situation, and to choose the one that makes us laugh. And spending time with our Dad, the soul of our family, has always been to understand that poor eyesight is not an obstacle to seeing what's important; good hearing is not a prerequisite for good listening; choosing not to speak is not the same as having nothing to say, one need but ask to hear it; and you don't need your own teeth to smile with joy.

We have 8 mm film that was converted for modern gadgets that our Mom narrated. She titled it, "The Frog Prince Lord, Mother Goose, and the Six Little Ducklings." Thus, the title line for these stories. We so hope that you have enjoyed spending time with us.

Our Mom once answered a question about what she'd like people to know about her by saying, "I tried." She commonly signed cards, "Peace, Love and Joy" and in spreading those, she entirely succeeded. We leave you now with the same sentiments. If her stories brought any or all of those your way, so too have we.

My Girls

They get a chance to do
What I'd had done
Had I a chance
When I was young.

— Ruth Lord

Other books by Roxanne:

FREE AIR-CONDITIONING WITH A POPCORN SCENT!

Kokopelli's Getaways with Happy
Authored as Lord Punchak
Written by Roxanne and illustrated by Marty

If You're Happy and You Know It, Wag Your Tale